MASTERPIECES

Written by Andrew Smithson

A TWOCAN PUBLICATION

©2016. Published by twocan under licence from West Ham United FC.

ISBN 978-1-911502-19-7

PICTURE CREDITS:
Action Images, Getty Images, Griffiths Photographers, Press Association, West Ham United FC.

6	Martin ALLEN	86	Frank LAMPARD Snr
8	Malcolm ALLISON	88	Andy MALCOLM
10	Yossi BENAYOUN	90	Alvin MARTIN
12	Slaven BILIC	94	Frank McAVENNIE
14	Ian BISHOP	98	Ludek MIKLOSKO
16	Billy BONDS	102	Bobby MOORE
20	Ronnie BOYCE	106	Malcolm MUSGROVE
22	Liam BRADY	108	Mark NOBLE
26	Trevor BROOKING	112	Graham PADDON
30	Ken BROWN	114	Scott PARKER
32	Johnny BYRNE	116	Phil PARKES
34	Noel CANTWELL	120	Dimitri PAYET
36	Michael CARRICK	122	Martin PETERS
38	Joe COLE	126	Geoff PIKE
40	Tony COTTEE	128	Steve POTTS
44	David CROSS	130	Bryan ROBSON
46	Brian DEAR	134	Alan SEALEY
48	Alan DEVONSHIRE	136	John SISSONS
52	Paolo DI CANIO	138	Jim STANDEN
56	John DICK	140	Ray STEWART
58	Julian DICKS		
62	Rio FERDINAND		
64	Tony GALE		
68	Paul GODDARD		
70	Ernie GREGORY		
72	John HARTSON		
74	Pat HOLLAND		
78	Geoff HURST		
82	Vic KEEBLE		
84	Frank LAMPARD Jnr		

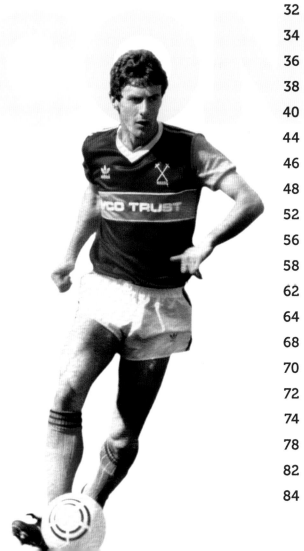

3

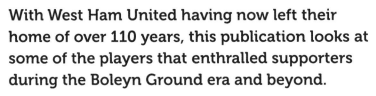

With West Ham United having now left their home of over 110 years, this publication looks at some of the players that enthralled supporters during the Boleyn Ground era and beyond.

With such a rich history, West Ham is one of the most iconic clubs in the country. Blessed with having had some of the best players the game has ever seen, Hammers fans have been treated to some exceptional talent and beautiful football through the decades and from the early years to the present day, they have always flocked in their numbers to get behind their heroes.

Pre-Second World War players, such as Jim Barrett, Len Goulden, Ted Hufton, George Kay, Billy Moore, Syd Puddefoot, Jimmy Ruffell, Danny Shea, Vic Watson and many more were idolised on the terraces, yet this book focuses on the period after that, during which football has grown into the global game it is now.

Some of the fifty men featured in this book were obvious choices and are unanimously hailed, but football, is of course, a game of opinions and there were a multitude of other Irons legends that could have easily been included.

Arguments could be made for example that Clyde Best, Mervyn Day, George Parris, Trevor Morley, Alan Taylor, Tommy Taylor, Phil Woosnam and Bobby Zamora to name but a few, were all worthy of attention, but the players included here, whether they were battling at the back, bossing midfield or spearheading the attack, are all Hammers Masterpieces...

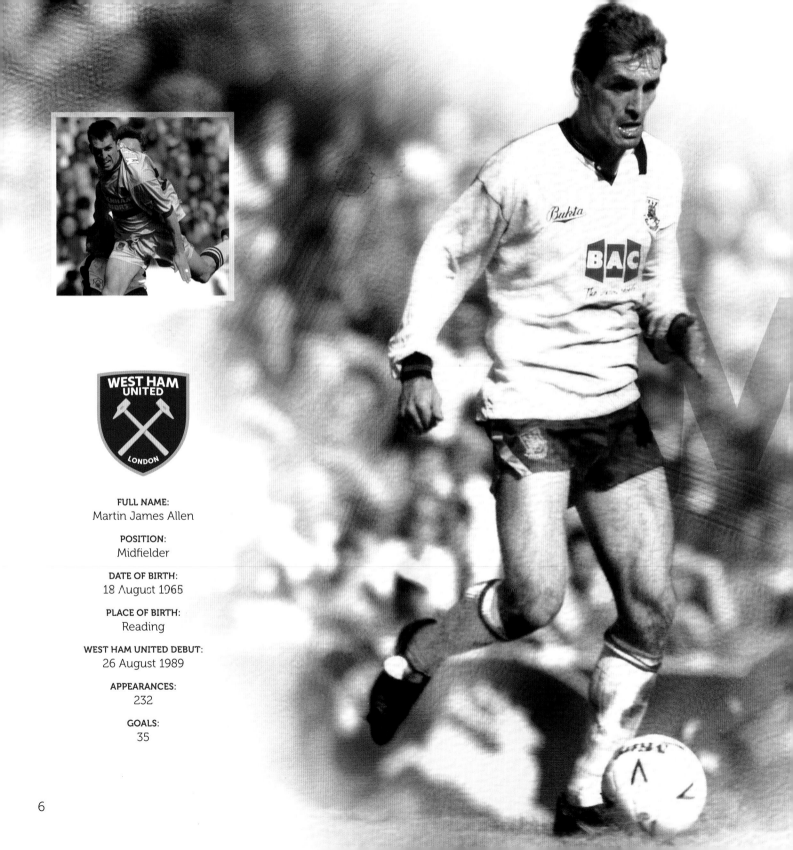

FULL NAME:
Martin James Allen

POSITION:
Midfielder

DATE OF BIRTH:
18 August 1965

PLACE OF BIRTH:
Reading

WEST HAM UNITED DEBUT:
26 August 1989

APPEARANCES:
232

GOALS:
35

Influential midfielder, Martin Allen became part of the new era at West Ham United when he joined from Queens Park Rangers as manager Lou Macari's first signing in 1989.

After scoring on his Hammers debut, a 3-2 Division Two victory over Plymouth Argyle, Allen quickly established himself as a first-team regular, despite Macari's departure in February 1990.

He played in the 1991 FA Cup semi-final loss to Nottingham Forest and was a vital part of the team that won promotion to Division One that year and, alongside Peter Butler, formed the midfield axis for the 1992/93 season, as the Hammers went up into the top flight again.

Allen's aggressive and determined style earned him the nickname of 'Mad Dog', but he was not just a destroyer. Runs of three goals in three games in January and then five goals in six games during April and May 1994 showed there was much more to his game, and by the time of his departure in 1995, West Ham had established themselves in the Premiership.

An England schoolboys international before later being capped at U21 level, Allen started his career at Queens Park Rangers, where he played in the 1986 League Cup final defeat to Oxford United. After his time at the Boleyn Ground he had spells at Portsmouth and Southend United before a move into management.

Among other appointments, he was assistant to Alan Pardew at his home-town club Reading and oversaw title-winning seasons at

ALLEN

Gillingham and Barnet, with whom he began a fourth stint in charge in March 2011.

One of three cousins to play for the Hammers alongside Paul and Clive, Allen's father, uncle and son have also played professionally.

One of the most innovative and recognisable coaches in the game, Malcolm Allison had been a stylish centre-half as a player.

A fringe member at Charlton Athletic for six years, he only made two league appearances for the Addicks, but soon became a regular at West Ham United after joining in February 1951, days after playing against them in a mid-season friendly.

Allison made his Hammers debut in an Essex Professional Cup semi-final against Leyton Orient, and after playing in the last ten Division Two fixtures, he ended the campaign with a winners' medal following a victory over Southend United in the final.

He was then the joint top appearance-maker in his first full season and occasionally filled in as a centre-forward, but West Ham remained a mid-table team for the majority of his time at the club.

By the time the Irons won Division Two in 1958, Allison had made his final professional appearance. He had started the campaign in the team, but took ill after defeat at Sheffield United in September 1957. He was diagnosed with tuberculosis.

Many of the foundations for promotion and the Club's future successes were accredited to Allison. He was a keen scholar of the game and as captain, influenced many of manager Ted Fenton's training regimes and tactics. He led coaching sessions with younger players too and helped bring Bobby Moore through the ranks.

ALLISON

Despite having a lung removed Allison battled his way back to fitness, but was unable to force his way into the side and was awarded a Testimonial against an All Star XI in November 1958. A brief spell at Southern League Romford followed in the early 1960s before he embarked on his illustrious managerial career.

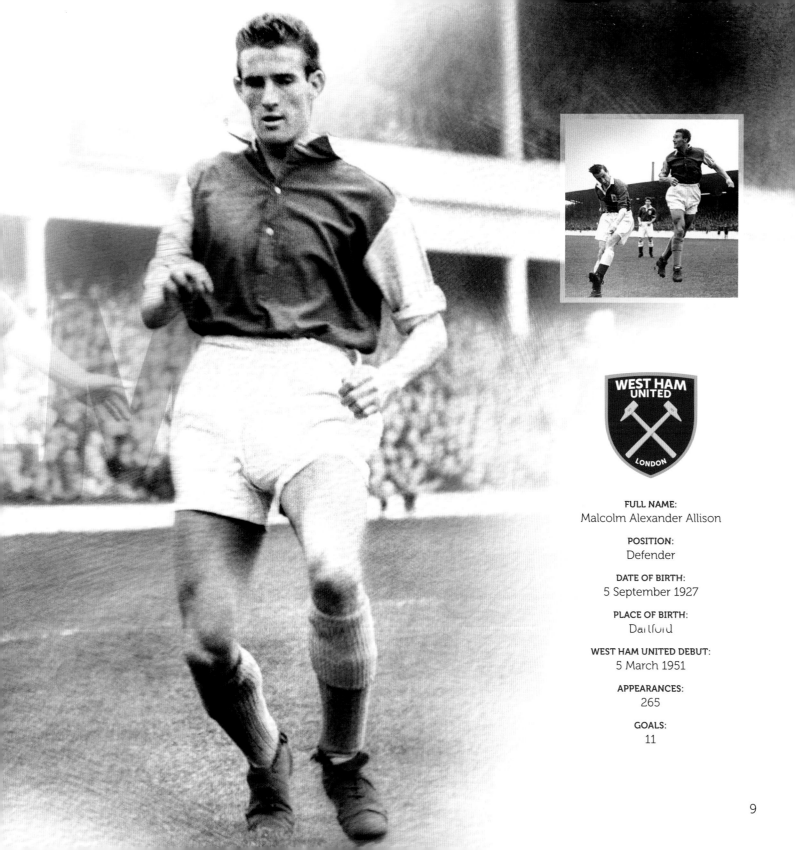

FULL NAME:
Malcolm Alexander Allison

POSITION:
Defender

DATE OF BIRTH:
5 September 1927

PLACE OF BIRTH:
Dartford

WEST HAM UNITED DEBUT:
5 March 1951

APPEARANCES:
265

GOALS:
11

Arriving at the club following West Ham United's Play-Off promotion to the Premier League in 2005, Yossi Benayoun's new manager Alan Pardew felt he was getting a player with the quality and ability to unlock a top-flight defence. He was soon proved right. The £2.5m signing adapted quickly to the pace of English game and after seven appearances had already scored twice.

After showing promise from an early age with Hapoel Be'er Sheva in his home country, Benayoun joined Ajax as a teenager. By the time he signed from Racing Santander, he was already an established Israel international and had broken his nation's appearance record.

With Benayoun's flair, the Hammers finished their first season back in a credible ninth place. It was in the FA Cup that they truly excelled however, with the Israeli playing in all but one game of the run, including the final against Liverpool.

Shortly before the cup final, he scored a late winner in the memorable 2-1 derby triumph over Tottenham Hotspur on the closing day of the league season. There had also been a winning goal in another derby win against Fulham earlier in the term. The team found things harder during the 2006/07 campaign and it was only on the last day that survival was ensured.

With relegation looming, Benayoun returned from injury for the final five fixtures - opening the scoring in the 3-0 win at Wigan Athletic and excelling with two vital blocks as Manchester United were dramatically beaten 1-0 at Old Trafford.

BENAYOUN

That was the final game of his first spell at the Boleyn Ground, but after moves to Liverpool and Chelsea, including a loan spell at Arsenal, he returned to the club on loan in August 2012. West Ham were again back in the Premier League, but with injury restricting him to just six appearances, he returned to Stamford Bridge.

An unused substitute in the 2013 UEFA Europa League final for Chelsea, he remained in the capital with Queens Park Rangers, before returning to his homeland for Maccabi Haifa in 2014.

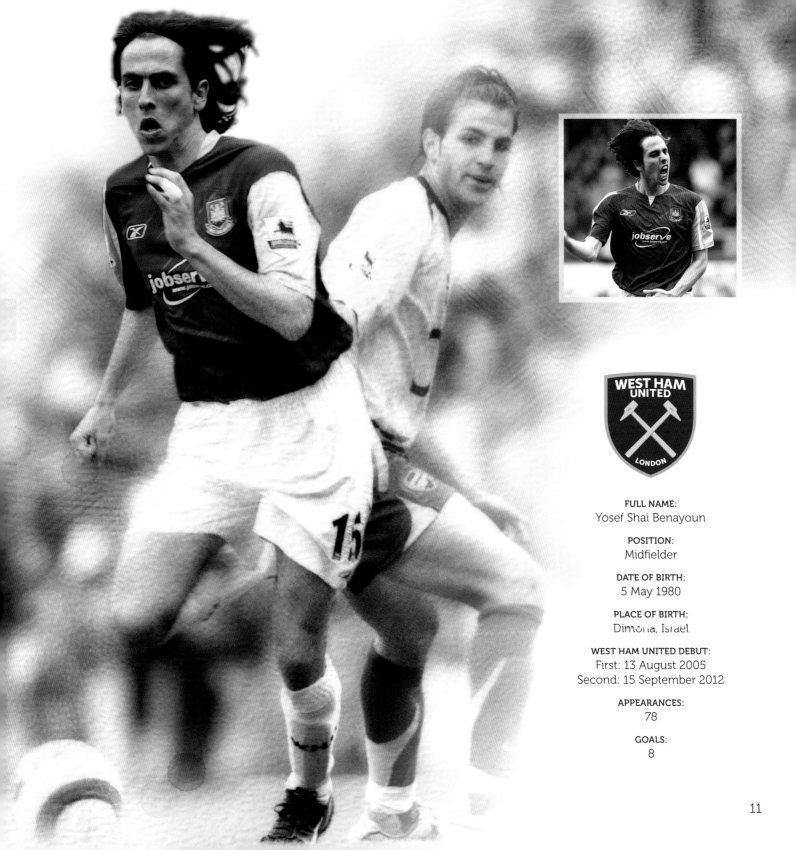

FULL NAME:
Yosef Shai Benayoun

POSITION:
Midfielder

DATE OF BIRTH:
5 May 1980

PLACE OF BIRTH:
Dimona, Israel

WEST HAM UNITED DEBUT:
First: 13 August 2005
Second: 15 September 2012

APPEARANCES:
78

GOALS:
8

FULL NAME:
Slaven Bilic

POSITION:
Defender

DATE OF BIRTH:
11 September 1968

PLACE OF BIRTH:
Split, Yugoslavia

WEST HAM UNITED DEBUT:
12 February 1996

APPEARANCES:
54

GOALS:
3

In June 2015, Slaven Bilic was tasked with guiding West Ham United through their final season at the Boleyn Ground, where he himself had starred almost 20 years earlier.

The Hammers broke their transfer record when matching a release clause in Bilic's contract with German outfit Karlsruher, where the defender had further enhanced his reputation since leaving his hometown club, Hajduk Split in 1993.

After four wins and a draw in his first five appearances, it quickly became apparent that he was a cool, yet rugged and passionate, defender who was never afraid of a tackle.

Bilic was a star for Croatia at UEFA Euro 96 as his country made their first finals appearance since breaking away from Yugoslavia, only going out at the quarter-final stage, narrowly beaten 2-1 by eventual tournament winners Germany.

The following campaign, 1996/97, was his only full season with West Ham. Everton agreed a deal to sign Bilic in March 1997, but only after it was decided that he could stay at the Boleyn Ground until the end of the campaign to help the Irons maintain their Premiership status. The Hammers finished in 14th place, two points above the drop zone and Bilic ended the season as Hammer of the Year runner-up.

A multi-lingual law graduate and an accomplished guitarist, Bilic's thorough management style saw an upturn in Croatia's results and performances during his six-year period at the helm.

BILIC

His tenure included equalling Croatia's tournament best finish by reaching the quarter-finals of Euro 2008.

Bilic's management career had started back at Hadjuk Split and again returning to a club he had played for, he emulated the man that brought him to West Ham, Harry Redknapp, and continued the club's fine tradition of former players taking charge.

FULL NAME:
Ian William Bishop

POSITION:
Midfielder

DATE OF BIRTH:
29 May 1965

PLACE OF BIRTH:
Liverpool

WEST HAM UNITED DEBUT:
30 December 1989

APPEARANCES:
304

GOALS:
17

With long flowing locks and the ability to spray the ball around, Liverpool-born Ian Bishop cut a dashing figure. A key part of West Ham United's engine room for seven years, his first few seasons at the club were never dull.

Following an injury to Julian Dicks, he took over the armband in his first full season, and skippered the side to promotion back to the top flight as runners-up to Oldham Athletic. Nine days after the end of that successful 1990/91 campaign, he debuted for England B at the Bescot Stadium in Walsall. He played his part in a 2-1 win over Switzerland B in a game where clubmate Stuart Slater also featured.

Relegation came the following season though and whilst Bishop was again influential in the club's 1992/93 promotion to the Premier League, there had been periods where he and several other players had been on the transfer list. Bishop had not been looking for a move away from the Boleyn Ground, but with their place in the top flight secured, he enjoyed more stability.

Under Billy Bonds, and then Harry Redknapp, Bishop provided the craft for four Premiership seasons, prior to his final appearance in a home 2-1 win over Chelsea in March 1998. He then moved back to Manchester City - the club he originally left to sign for West Ham.

Bishop had come through the ranks at Everton as a youngster and after a loan spell with Crewe Alexandra, made his mark at Carlisle United.

BISHOP

A first meeting with Redknapp at Bournemouth for a season, led to his first arrival at Maine Road and in his second spell the Sky Blues earned successive promotions.

In the final years of his career, he worked with a couple of former teammates, playing under Kenny Brown at Barry Town and then working as an assistant manager to fellow Liverpudlian Mike Marsh, at Burscough.

A true club legend, Billy Bonds is one of only two players to have been awarded two Testimonials at the Boleyn Ground - coincidentally, his first game for the club over 20 years before, had been in a testimonial for someone else.

Although his full debut came in the 1967/68 season opener against Sheffield Wednesday, Hammers fans first got a glimpse of their new marauding right-back a few months earlier, turning out against a Select XI on behalf of Ken Brown.

A crowd of almost 15,000 witnessed Bonds settling into his new surroundings, shortly after arriving from Charlton Athletic, for whom he had made almost 100 appearances. That total was dwarfed by the all-time appearance record he set for West Ham United, as the £50,000 outlay made by Ron Greenwood was paid back in spades.

Later, he moved into midfield and then central defence, Bonds was versatile. He was brave in the tackle and would regularly play through the pain barrier, but there was much more to his game. Bonds always used the ball well, he could take a mean penalty, and in the 1973/74 season, when he first became captain, his 13 goals made him joint top scorer and went a long way to ensuring the side avoided relegation.

His haul included a virtuoso hat-trick in the 3-0 defeat of Chelsea and the points proved vital. The team only won two further games as they edged towards safety, yet 12 months later Bonds was being presented with the FA Cup.

BONDS

When Bobby Moore left for eventual cup final opponents Fulham two months before the win over Chelsea, Bonds, who always lead by example, was the natural successor to the captaincy.

He was first voted Hammer of the Year in 1971, when his dependable displays had again steered the club from relegation. He won the honour three times in five years and for a final fourth time during the later years of his distinguished career in 1987.

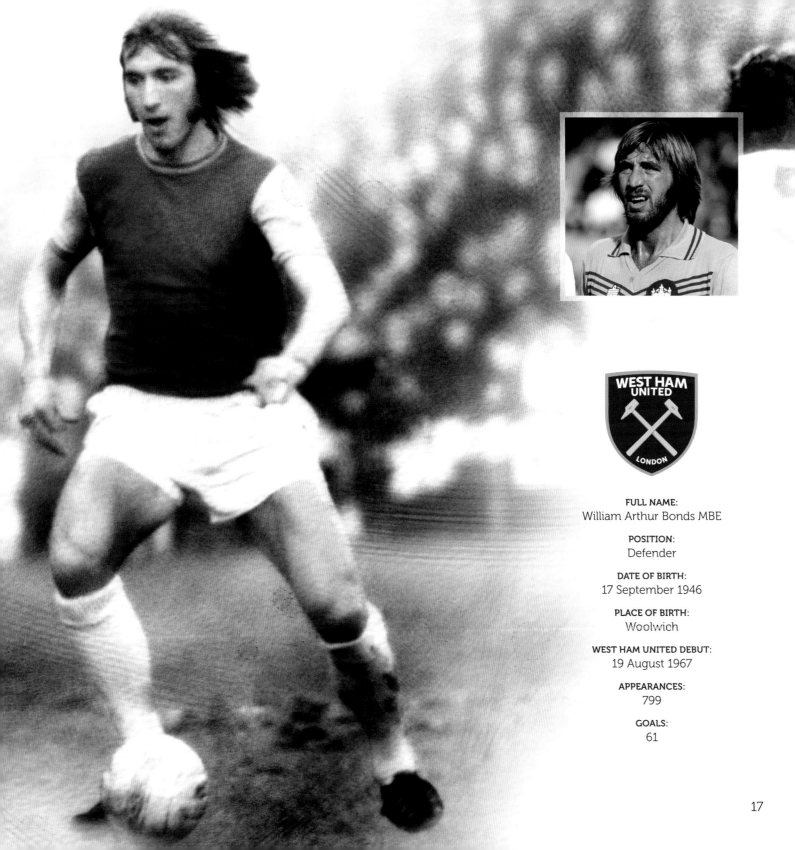

FULL NAME:
William Arthur Bonds MBE

POSITION:
Defender

DATE OF BIRTH:
17 September 1946

PLACE OF BIRTH:
Woolwich

WEST HAM UNITED DEBUT:
19 August 1967

APPEARANCES:
799

GOALS:
61

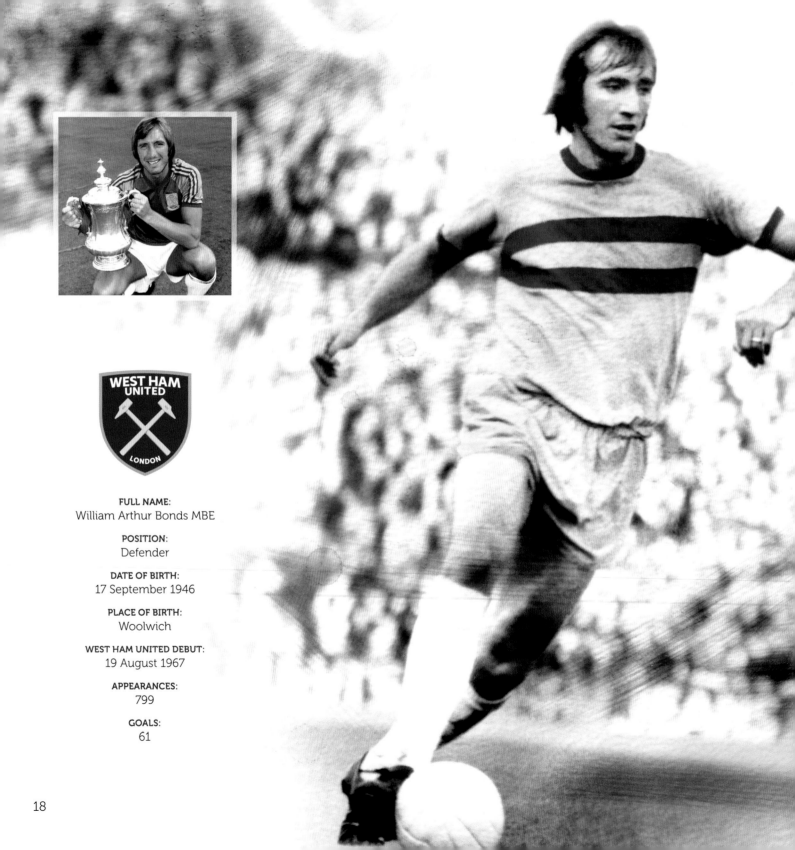

FULL NAME:
William Arthur Bonds MBE

POSITION:
Defender

DATE OF BIRTH:
17 September 1946

PLACE OF BIRTH:
Woolwich

WEST HAM UNITED DEBUT:
19 August 1967

APPEARANCES:
799

GOALS:
61

The 1975 FA Cup win over Fulham was followed by an exhilarating run to the 1976 UEFA Cup Winners' Cup final. West Ham lost to Anderlecht, but these were glory years for the Irons and despite relegation to Division Two in 1978, he was soon to guide the club to another two cup finals and a successful promotion charge.

Bonds galvanised the Hammers and in 1980, after a 1-0 victory over the Gunners, he again lifted the FA Cup, before being presented with the Division Two winners' trophy in 1981. This was his 13th season at the Boleyn Ground and with 59 appearances, the most he made in one campaign, he still going strong.

West Ham's defence of the FA Cup ended early, but they reached the quarter-finals of the Cup Winners' Cup and took Liverpool to a replay in the League Cup final. With Bonds imperious at the back, the side did not lose a league match after December and Division Two was won by 13 points.

The club steadied the ship in Division One and having already reached Moore's record appearance mark, Bonds was supposed to retire in 1984. It did not last long, injuries saw him fill a number of positions during 1984/85 and while his own toe problem meant he sat out the following campaign, Bonds did not end his career until 30 April 1988 with a loss at Southampton.

John Lyall's offer to coach the youth team set Bonds on a path that led to his appointment as manager in February 1990.

BONDS

That same year the Boleyn Ground hosted a second testimonial for 'Bonzo'. As in 1978, Tottenham Hotspur were the opponents and on both occasions the main man scored from the spot. Memorable occasions both, for a Hammers great who had been awarded an MBE in 1988 and in 2013 was presented the club's first Lifetime Achievement Award.

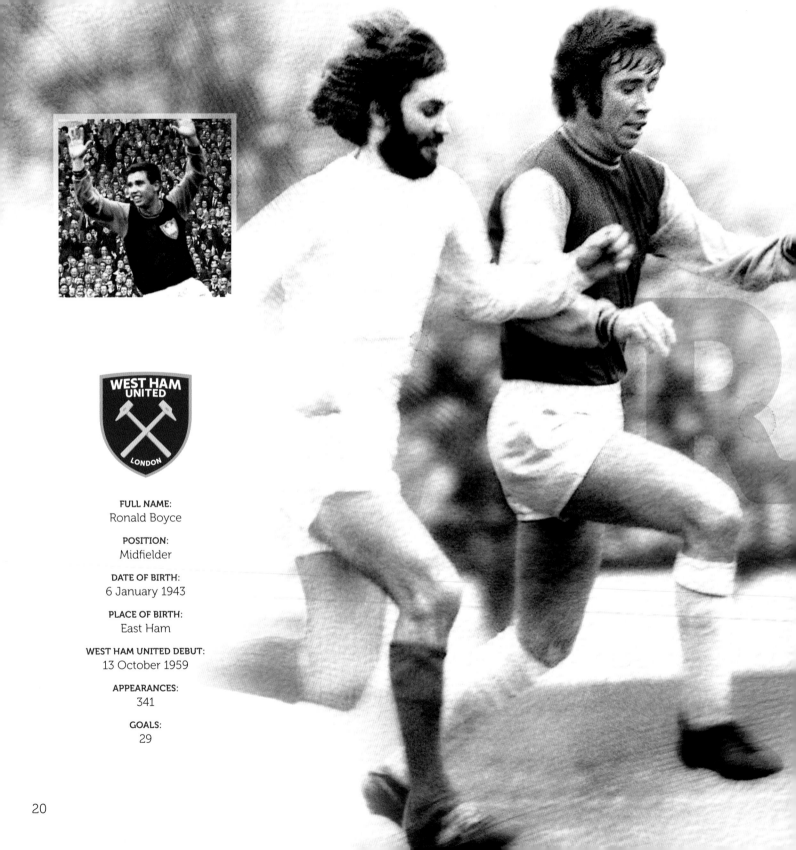

FULL NAME:
Ronald Boyce

POSITION:
Midfielder

DATE OF BIRTH:
6 January 1943

PLACE OF BIRTH:
East Ham

WEST HAM UNITED DEBUT:
13 October 1959

APPEARANCES:
341

GOALS:
29

From being on the ground staff to scoring the winner in the FA Cup Final, Ronnie Boyce lived his boyhood dream.

A one-club man, Boyce had a distinguished career in the famous claret and blue following his debut in the Southern Floodlight Cup against Millwall. An understudy to many, it was just over a year before his next first team appearance, but after his first real run in the side during the 1962/63 campaign, he never looked back.

Boyce missed only two games during the following two seasons, as West Ham United won their first major honours. Two goals in the 3-1 FA Cup semi-final victory over Manchester United and then the last-gasp winner against Preston North End in the final guaranteed his place in Hammers folklore, but Boyce was far from done.

His headed goal against La Gantoise and his superb performance against Sparta Prague in the first two rounds of the following season's UEFA Cup Winners' Cup, paved the way for West Ham's return to the twin towers of Wembley and victory against TSV Munich 1860.

In 1966, the club reached the League Cup final and the semi-final in their defence of the Cup Winners' Cup. Boyce was an essential part of that great cup team, yet some of his best work went unseen. An unselfish, tireless performer, he was seen as the heartbeat of the team and as such, was presented with a watch at his testimonial in 1972, in reference to his nickname 'Ticker'.

BOYCE

The game against Manchester United was held a month after Boyce's retirement. His final goal had been almost two years prior, when he superbly volleyed home a Joe Corrigan clearance from the edge of the centre circle, showing all the technique of a player that had represented England Schoolboys and been a talented cricketer as a youth. He went on to become an integral member of the Irons' backroom staff for another two decades.

Liam Brady played in West Ham United's 1980 FA Cup Final triumph, although on that day, he was wearing the yellow and blue away colours of Arsenal.

The match was one of the Irishman's final appearances for the Gunners prior to his move to Italy. A firm fans' favourite at Highbury, Brady was a huge success following his arrival as a schoolboy in 1971.

The Hammers were hosting Burnley across the capital when Brady made his senior bow for Arsenal, a substitute in a 1-0 victory over Birmingham City. While with the north london club, he was selected for the PFA Team of the year in three consecutive seasons. He won the PFA Player of the year award outright for 1978/79, when he helped Arsenal lift the FA Cup, beating Manchester United 3-2 in a thrilling Wembley final.

The defeat to West Ham at Wembley twelve months later was Brady's third final in a row, but it was not the only time he came up against the Irons with silverware at stake. In May 1977, the two clubs met in the final of the London Five-A-Side Football Championship, next door to the twin towers at the Empire Pool. The format suited Brady's close control and dribbling skills and he scored both goals in a 2-1 win as West Ham lost the final for a third time in six years, having last won it in 1970.

Four days after losing to West Ham in the FA Cup, Arsenal also lost the UEFA Cup Winners' Cup final against Valencia. Brady was at ease

BRADY

playing European football and having impressed against Juventus in the semi-final, made the move to Serie A in the summer of 1980.

At Juve, he won two league titles, scoring the goal that secured the 1982 Scudetto against Catanzaro, before also playing for Sampdoria, Inter Milan and Ascoli.

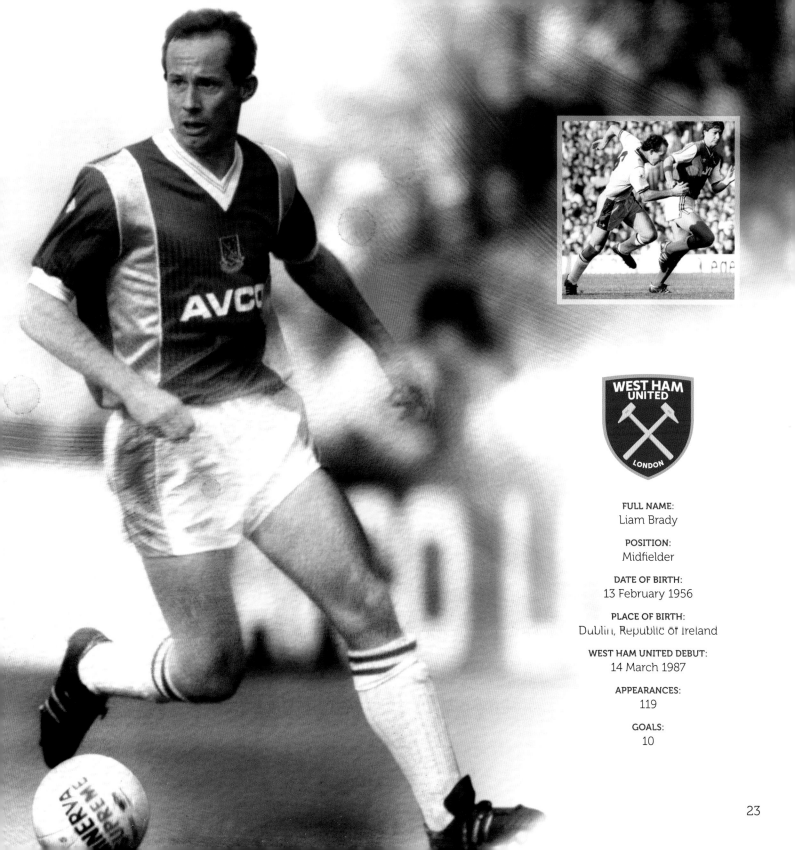

WEST HAM UNITED
LONDON

FULL NAME:
Liam Brady

POSITION:
Midfielder

DATE OF BIRTH:
13 February 1956

PLACE OF BIRTH:
Dublin, Republic of Ireland

WEST HAM UNITED DEBUT:
14 March 1987

APPEARANCES:
119

GOALS:
10

Brady's return to England in 1987, when he signed for John Lyall at West Ham, was much heralded, and his elegant passing game and superb technical ability was still clear for the Boleyn Ground faithful to see.

He did not have to wait long for his first goal for the club, scoring in a 3-1 win in his fifth appearance - almost inevitably against his old club Arsenal, but eleven months after joining, he suffered knee ligament damage at Derby County and was sidelined for nine months.

Brady came back with a bang, returning to the side in a League Cup tie against the same opponents. The Rams were hammered 5-0. The Irons went nap again in his second game on the comeback trail, West Bromwich Albion were dispatched 5-2 in the Full Members Cup.

With Brady back, West Ham reached the FA Cup quarter-finals and League Cup semi-finals, but their League form was poor. The side were already in deep relegation trouble and after falling into the bottom two following a defeat to Luton Town on Brady's league return, they never escaped the drop-zone. His deft touches and subtle moves were some of the bright spots of the campaign, but Brady's final season of football was to be played in Division Two.

The club again reached the League Cup semi-finals and adapted to the second tier reasonably well, but one of the season's undoubted highlights came on the final day. Brady capped his last game for the Hammers with a tremendous strike, sealing a 4-0 triumph over Wolverhampton Wanderers at the Boleyn Ground.

BRADY

Brady won eleven caps for the Republic of Ireland while with West Ham. He later worked under Giovanni Trappattoni, the man that took him to Juventus, as assistant manager to the national side. A manager at Celtic and Brighton & Hove Albion too, he spent 18 years back at Arsenal overseeing their successful youth system.

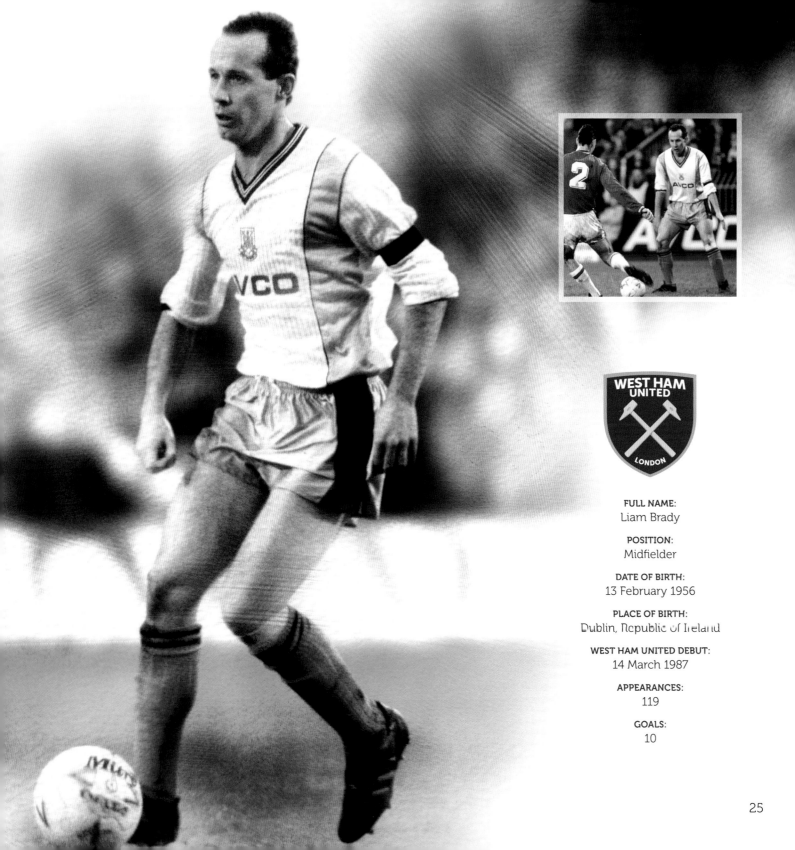

FULL NAME:
Liam Brady

POSITION:
Midfielder

DATE OF BIRTH:
13 February 1956

PLACE OF BIRTH:
Dublin, Republic of Ireland

WEST HAM UNITED DEBUT:
14 March 1987

APPEARANCES:
119

GOALS:
10

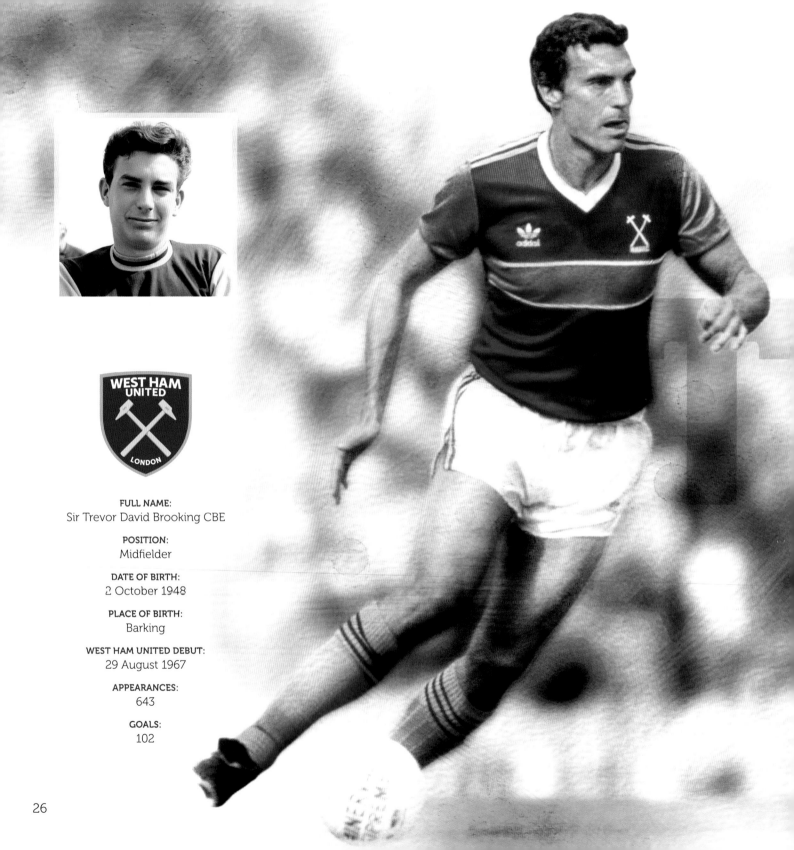

FULL NAME:
Sir Trevor David Brooking CBE

POSITION:
Midfielder

DATE OF BIRTH:
2 October 1948

PLACE OF BIRTH:
Barking

WEST HAM UNITED DEBUT:
29 August 1967

APPEARANCES:
643

GOALS:
102

A Knight and a gentleman, throughout his long career in football, Sir Trevor Brooking has carried himself with great dignity and is widely regarded one of the club's greatest ever players.

When Brooking joined West Ham United in 1965, it was on the condition that he could continue his school studies and having gained his qualifications, he made his league debut two years later.

Brooking was an orthodox striker in his early days, and while he is one of only ten men to score more than a century of goals for the Hammers, he was largely a bit-part player in that role, despite a hat-trick in his first season during a 5-0 rout of Newcastle United.

It was in the 1971/72 campaign, following a move into midfield, that Brooking came into his own, at the club he had supported as a boy. He still displayed a keen eye for goal, but from the centre of the park he could read the game and picked holes in opposition defences for the next twelve years.

Supporters appreciated, not only Brooking's style, but how he conducted himself both on and off the pitch. He played to the whistle and lived a professional lifestyle, winning the Hammer of the Year award on five occasions and finishing runner-up a further three times. The first in 1972, came at the end of his first campaign as a regular, he then took the prize three seasons on the spin between 1976 and 1978 and again in 1984.

BROOKING

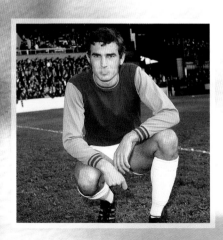

Those were difficult years for the Irons. In 1975, Brooking was part of the FA Cup winning side, his goal in the fourth round replay against Swindon Town helping them on their way, but following defeat in the UEFA Cup Winners' Cup final, league form slipped and the club were relegated at the end of 1977/78.

Brooking remained at the Boleyn Ground following the drop, having already enjoyed a testimonial against an England XI managed by Ron Greenwood in 1977.

Greenwood had given Brooking his Hammers' debut and remained at the club when Brooking earned his first England cap in 1974, but that night his team lost 6-2 to the Hammers.

In 1980, West Ham became only the eighth second tier club to lift the FA Cup. After another vital replay goal, this time against West Bromwich Albion, Brooking was the match winner in the final, his first-half header seeing off Arsenal. The FA Cup was won for the second time in six seasons and Brooking had played in all but one match of the cup-winning runs.

In 1976, his goals against Eintracht Frankfurt had put West Ham into the UEFA Cup Winners' Cup final and in the marathon 1980/81 season, they not only reached the third round of the same competition, but Brooking dominated, as the club coasted to the Division Two title. Following his second Charity Shield appearance, he returned to Wembley again for the League Cup final against Liverpool, only to be narrowly beaten 2-1 in the Villa Park replay.

Brooking was no stranger to big England games either. Shortly after his cup-final winner, he netted the first in a 2-0 victory over Scotland in the British Home Championship and again scored the opener in the UEFA Euro 1980 2-1 win against Spain. His final international goals came in June 1981, scoring twice as England beat Hungary 3-1 to qualify for the 1982 FIFA World Cup.

BROOKING

Brooking played Sunday League football after retiring and remains heavily involved in sport, holding several high ranking administrative roles within the Football Association and other organisations.

His 1981 MBE was elevated to CBE in 1999 and in 2004, Brooking was knighted for his services to sport. A year earlier, he was twice caretaker manager at the Boleyn Ground, where in 2009, the Centenary Stand was renamed after him.

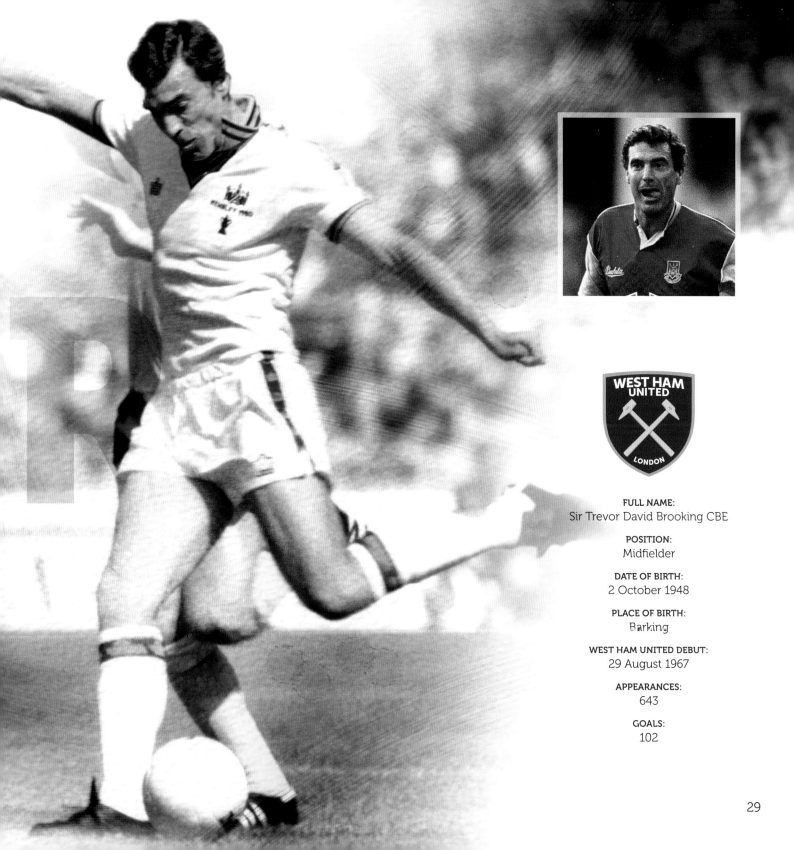

FULL NAME:
Sir Trevor David Brooking CBE

POSITION:
Midfielder

DATE OF BIRTH:
2 October 1948

PLACE OF BIRTH:
Barking

WEST HAM UNITED DEBUT:
29 August 1967

APPEARANCES:
643

GOALS:
102

FULL NAME:
Kenneth Brown

POSITION:
Defender

DATE OF BIRTH:
16 February 1932

PLACE OF BIRTH:
Forest Gate

WEST HAM UNITED DEBUT:
21 February 1953

APPEARANCES:
474

GOALS:
4

Long-serving Ken Brown was a popular figure at the Boleyn Ground, but first and foremost he was a very dependable performer.

Local boy Brown joined West Ham United via non-league football and after two years in the reserves, made his professional debut shortly after his 21st birthday.

By the start of the 1957/58 campaign he was firmly ensconced at the heart of the Hammers' defence and missed only one game as West Ham secured the Division Two title. The following season, after helping the Hammers match their then highest Division One finish, the ever-present Brown was named Hammer of the Year.

Brown was now an integral part of the side. He missed only two games in 1959/60 and was again an ever-present in 1960/61. There was an England cap too. In 1959 he played in the Home International Championship 2-1 victory against Northern Ireland at Wembley.

Two further Wembley appearances secured Brown's place in West Ham history. He played in every game of both the 1964 FA Cup and 1965 UEFA Cup Winners' Cup successes, including the finals.

Brown was an out-and-out defender, scoring only four goals. The first, nine years after debuting, in a 5-0 defeat of Birmingham City. Conversely, when Brown's son Kenny joined the Hammers, his first goal was against the Blues' second city rivals Aston Villa.

BROWN

Kenny was born shortly after his father left the Irons following a Testimonial in 1967. When Brown senior retired from playing three seasons later, he went into management, guiding Norwich City to 1985 League Cup glory.

The arrival of Johnny Byrne at the Boleyn Ground was a real sign of intent from West Ham United manager Ron Greenwood.

A record fee between two English clubs of £65,000 was agreed with Crystal Palace to bring Byrne to the club, with the deal seeing Ron Brett going the other way.

There was another clause in the transfer allowing him to return to Palace a few weeks later to play in a high-profile friendly against Spanish giants Real Madrid, but after working so hard to bring Byrne into the squad, he did not disappoint.

Byrne had been recommended to the Glaziers by Vincent Blore, who played for the Hammers as a goalkeeper between 1935 and 1936. Byrne made his senior debut in 1956 at Selhurst Park and was a key member of the 1960/61 promotion success when Palace finished runners-up in Division Four.

That season also saw Byrne achieve the rare feat of playing for England despite not being in one of the top two divisions. While at West Ham his international career continued, including a hat-trick in Lisbon, as England overpowered a Eusébio-inspired Portugal, 4-3.

Hammer of the Year in 1964, Byrne formed a deadly partnership with Geoff Hurst. Goals against Leyton Orient, Swindon Town and Burnley helped the club to the FA Cup that year, and while he missed the subsequent UEFA Cup Winners' Cup final, his goals were again invaluable on the run to success.

BYRNE

He did feature in the 1966 League Cup final however, scoring in the first leg, and although West Bromwich Albion lifted the trophy, he was unstoppable in the same competition the following season - assisting all seven goals in the thrashing of Leeds United.

A cool penalty taker, Byrne returned to Palace in 1967 having scored better than a goal every two games for the Irons. A year later he joined Fulham before finishing his career in South Africa, playing for and then managing Durban City, before spending most of his coaching career at Cape Town club Hellenic.

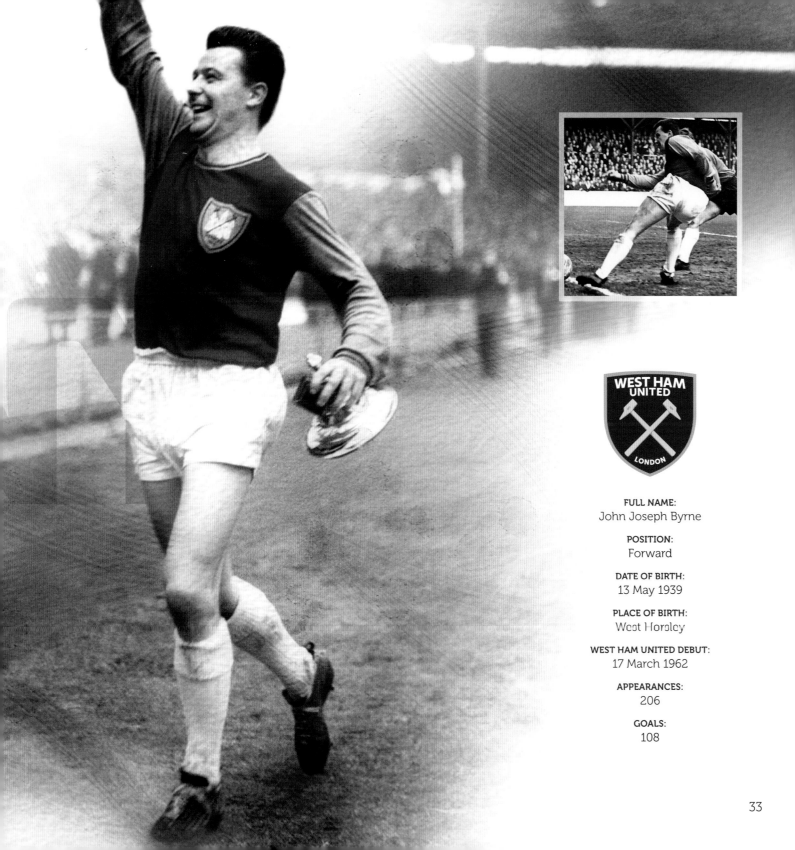

FULL NAME:
John Joseph Byrne

POSITION:
Forward

DATE OF BIRTH:
13 May 1939

PLACE OF BIRTH:
West Horsley

WEST HAM UNITED DEBUT:
17 March 1962

APPEARANCES:
206

GOALS:
108

FULL NAME:
Noel Euchuria Cornelius Cantwell

POSITION:
Defender

DATE OF BIRTH:
28 February 1932

PLACE OF BIRTH:
Cork, Republic of Ireland

WEST HAM UNITED DEBUT:
13 November 1952

APPEARANCES:
278

GOALS:
12

Swashbuckling full-back Noel Cantwell, was as dashing off the pitch as he was attractive to watch on it, his attacking style hinting that he had originally been a striker when he arrived at West Ham United.

Cantwell was playing in his home town of Cork when he was scouted by the Hammers. Cork Athletic staged their games at the Mardyke Sports Ground and to recognise his vast achievements after his death in 2005, a street in the same district was later named after him.

Following his arrival in London, Cantwell swiftly dropped into defence. His debut came in an Essex Professional Cup tie victory over Colchester United and a month later he helped West Ham win the London FA Challenge Cup against Brentford.

There were other minor honours in the form of the Southern Floodlight Cup in 1956 and the last ever Essex Professional Cup in 1959, but Cantwell also enjoyed more significant success while at the Boleyn Ground, representing his country both at football and cricket and skippering his club to the 1957/58 Division Two title.

Cantwell oozed authority and was obvious captain material, taking the armband at Old Trafford too following a record-breaking move to Manchester United in 1960. One of the most recognisable players in the game, he won two league titles and the FA Cup during his time with the Red Devils.

Having served for a period as Chairman of the Professional Footballers Association, Cantwell seamlessly moved into management following

CANTWELL

his retirement. In his first post at Coventry City he qualified for the Inter-Cities Fairs Cup, a tournament in which he had previously represented London while at West Ham.

He took Peterborough United to the Division Four title in 1973/74, and after enjoying roles in the North American Soccer League with the New England Tea Men and the Jacksonville Tea Men, he returned to London Road in 1986 before his retirement from the game.

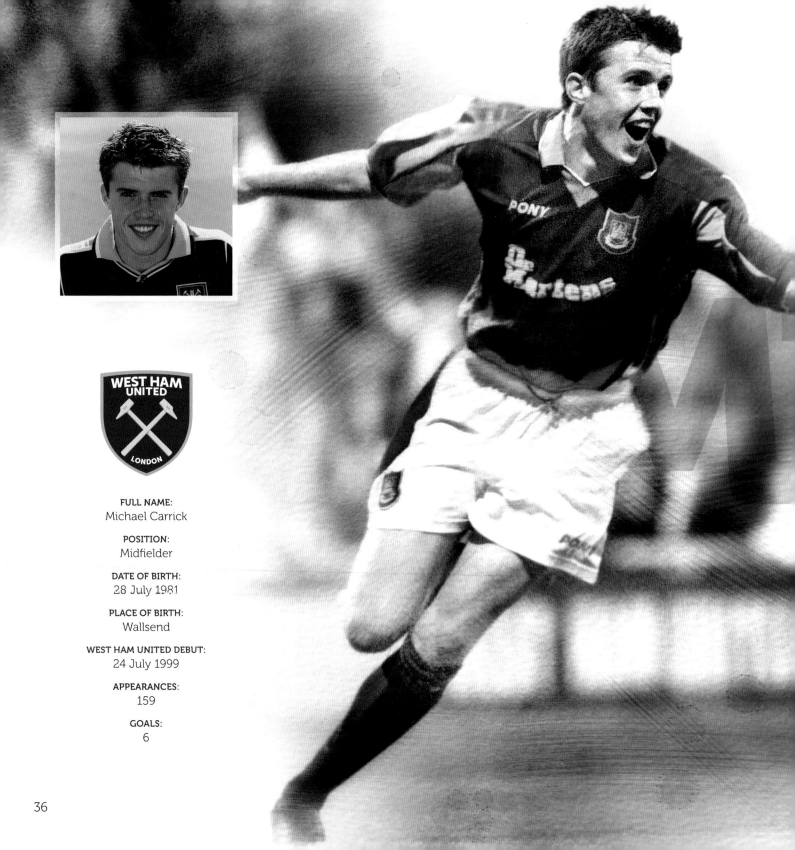

WEST HAM UNITED
LONDON

FULL NAME:
Michael Carrick

POSITION:
Midfielder

DATE OF BIRTH:
28 July 1981

PLACE OF BIRTH:
Wallsend

WEST HAM UNITED DEBUT:
24 July 1999

APPEARANCES:
159

GOALS:
6

The youngest person to sign professional forms for West Ham United since the 1920s, Michael Carrick was one of the famed Academy of Football's many products to reach the very top.

Nurtured by Tony Carr and his staff, Carrick was originally a striker, but developed into an intelligent midfielder. An old head on young shoulders, never flustered in possession, his style set him apart from other players and saw him pull the strings from deep for the Hammers.

Carrick's debut came at the start of 1999/00, after starring the previous season in the fantastic 9-0 aggregate FA Youth Cup final victory over Coventry City, the same club he later scored his first senior goal against. He twice went on loan during his first senior season too, first to Swindon Town and then Birmingham City. Once back at the Boleyn, Carrick cemented his first-team place and ended his first season as Hammers' Young Player of the Year.

Having already represented England at U18 and U21 levels, he quickly progressed to the senior squad. His full debut came in a comprehensive 4-0 win over Mexico at Pride Park in May 2001 and it was while on international duty in 2003, that he picked up an injury that was to have major consequences.

Now wearing the number six on his back, having formerly been squad number 21, Carrick's previous domestic appearance was a 2-0 win over Sunderland that kept the Hammers just above the relegation zone. Unavailable for the 2002/03 run-in however, he looked on as the club

CARRICK

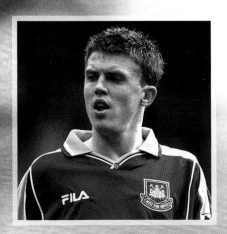

failed to beat the drop and were forced to sell several players. Sticking with the club for another year, his final game for the Irons was at the Millennium Stadium for the Play-Off final defeat by Crystal Palace. That summer, Carrick moved to Tottenham Hotspur, who weeks before his England injury, he had scored against in a 2-0 win.

After two seasons at White Hart Lane, he moved to Manchester United, winning a host of trophies including the 2008 UEFA Champions League.

WEST HAM UNITED
LONDON

FULL NAME:
Joseph John Cole

POSITION:
Midfielder

DATE OF BIRTH:
8 November 1981

PLACE OF BIRTH:
Islington

WEST HAM UNITED DEBUT:
First: 2 January 1999
Second: 5 January 2013

APPEARANCES:
187

GOALS:
18

Boy-wonder, Joe Cole was the talk of English football when he broke into West Ham United's first team.

A product of the club's prolific youth system, Cole caught the eye playing for his country at schoolboy level and was soon being compared with some of the most skilful players in the game.

Only 17 when he came on against Swansea City in the FA Cup, another of Cole's early appearances was as a substitute against Metz, in the second leg of the UEFA Intertoto Cup final at the start of the 1999/00 campaign.

The Irons won 3-2 on aggregate and at the end of the season, Cole was voted Young Hammer of the Year. Versatile and full of tricks, he won the senior award in 2003, but with the club relegated that season they were forced to sell their star man.

At Chelsea, Cole won all three major domestic trophies and became an England regular. He had already made his full international debut while still at the Boleyn Ground, coming on during the 4-0 friendly victory over Mexico in 2001, alongside fellow academy graduate and FA Youth Cup winning teammate Michael Carrick.

He left Stamford Bridge for Liverpool and then enjoyed a season -long loan at Lille before reportedly taking a pay cut to make an emotional return to West Ham in 2013. In his second spell he had an important part in helping the club re-establish themselves back in the Premier League, having been promoted the previous summer.

COLE

He netted the first goal of the 2013/14 season as West Ham beat Cardiff City 2-0 and although he was released at the end of the campaign, he remained in claret and blue following a move to Aston Villa before subsequently joining near -neighbours Coventry City in 2015.

A forward with the knack of being in the right place at the right time, Tony Cottee started his football career with a bang and never looked back.

Scoring on his West Ham United debut in a 3-0 win over Tottenham Hotspur on New Year's Day 1983, he enjoyed a run of seven goals in his first ten appearances. He ended the 1982/83 campaign with a brace in a 4-2 triumph at Coventry City and started the next with another, in the 4-0 beating of Birmingham City at the Boleyn.

Now firmly established in the first team, two months later he grabbed four goals as Bury were crushed 10-0 in the League Cup, the first of five occasions during his first stint with the Hammers where he went home with the match ball. Hat-tricks followed against Wimbledon in 1985, within a month of each other in 1986 against Queens Park Rangers and Preston North End, and at Coventry in 1987.

In his first two full seasons, Cottee was top scorer, but the team's form fluctuated wildly. 1985/86 saw them come close to title glory though, eventually finishing third in Division One and while Frank McAvennie outscored him, the pair were almost unstoppable.

During September and October of 1985 alone, Cottee scored in seven consecutive appearances and had a run of ten goals in ten games. His form saw him named Hammer of Year, having finished runner-up the two seasons prior, and also PFA Young Player of the Year.

COTTEE

Cottee scored twice in the final against KV Mechelen as West Ham warmed up for the following season by winning the Groningen Tournament, but while he remained in the goals, the team struggled to reproduce their title-challenging form. During 1986/87, he was ever-present, regaining his top scorer mantle in the process.

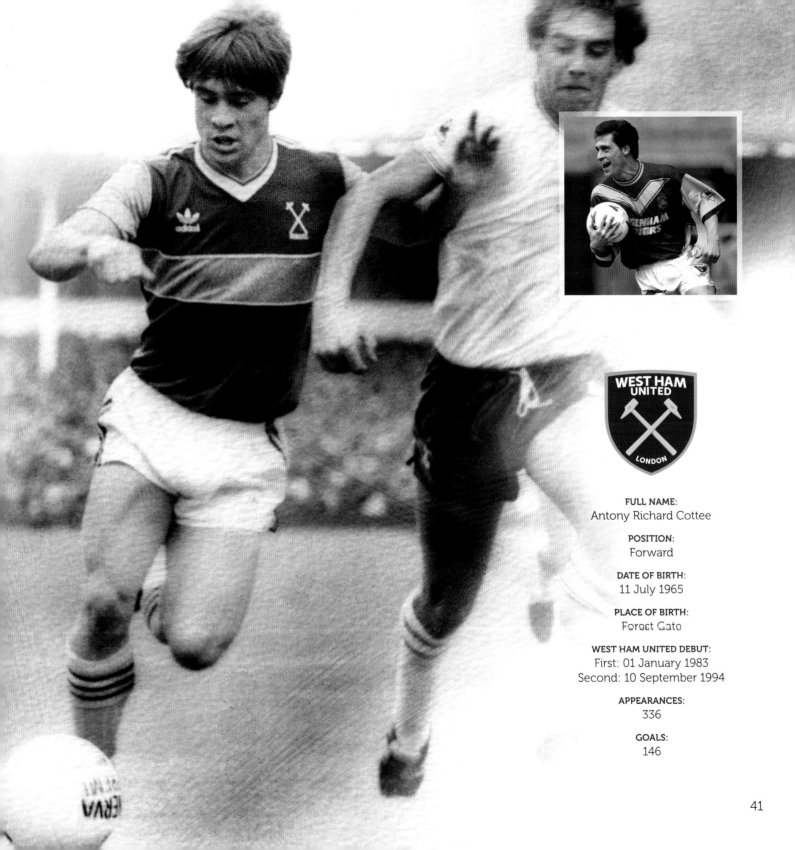

FULL NAME:
Antony Richard Cottee

POSITION:
Forward

DATE OF BIRTH:
11 July 1965

PLACE OF BIRTH:
Forest Gate

WEST HAM UNITED DEBUT:
First: 01 January 1983
Second: 10 September 1994

APPEARANCES:
336

GOALS:
146

FULL NAME:
Antony Richard Cottee

POSITION:
Forward

DATE OF BIRTH:
11 July 1965

PLACE OF BIRTH:
Forest Gate

WEST HAM UNITED DEBUT:
First: 01 January 1983
Second: 10 September 1994

APPEARANCES:
336

GOALS:
146

Cottee made his full England debut in September 1986, coming on as a second-half replacement for John Barnes in the 1-0 defeat to Sweden in Stockholm. It was the first of three caps earned while a Hammer. Cottee also played for England U21s eight times during his time at the Boleyn Ground.

His debut at U21 level was in 1984, when teammate Alan Dickens also played in a win over Finland at the Dell, and Cottee's first goal for the U21s came after he had turned out for the seniors, when he scored the winner in a 2-1 victory in Spain in February 1987.

The following year saw West Ham accept a British record transfer fee from Everton for Cottee, who became a popular figure at Goodison Park. Again, he was regularly on the scoresheet, but with the side never fully clicking over a prolonged period, he made a very welcome return to the Irons in 1994.

Having been sent off in his second debut for the club, away at Liverpool, Cottee made amends by scoring in his first game back on home soil, getting the only goal of the game against Aston Villa. Before the year was out he grabbed another hat-trick, this time scoring all three in the 3-0 victory over Manchester City, and at the end of the season was once again runner-up in the Hammer of the Year awards.

West Ham flirted with relegation before pulling away to safety late on, and in 1995/96 they were steady throughout with Cottee taking up his customary place at the top of the team's scoring charts for both campaigns.

COTTEE

Early the following season, having comfortably secured his position in the club's top ten all-time scorers list, Cottee moved on. The destination, Selangor, helping the Red Giants win the Malaysia FA Cup. Upon his return to England, he joined Leicester City, picking up a League Cup winners' medal in 2000, after the Foxes' 2-1 victory over Tranmere Rovers.

A player-coach at Norwich City and then player-manager at Barnet, his final competitive appearances were with London rivals Millwall.

FULL NAME:
David Cross

POSITION:
Forward

DATE OF BIRTH:
8 December 1950

PLACE OF BIRTH:
Heywood

WEST HAM UNITED DEBUT:
17 December 1977

APPEARANCES:
224

GOALS:
97

David Cross had a somewhat nomadic football career, playing for 13 different clubs, but the team he made the most appearances for was, comfortably, West Ham United.

Cross was an old-school target man and his willingness to put himself about and work a shift was fully appreciated by the Boleyn faithful, players and staff alike. When manager John Lyall asked him to play the lone striker role in the 1980 FA Cup final, he knew exactly what he would be getting, and it proved to be a major factor in the win over Arsenal.

The cup success was in Cross' second full season with the Hammers. He arrived from West Bromwich Albion as a club record signing half way through the 1977/78 campaign, but with the side already in relegation trouble, his role in helping the Hammers clinch the Division Two title in 1980/81 was invaluable.

Top scorer in the division, nine years after he had originally won the Division Two title with Norwich City, Cross also played in the season's Charity Shield and League Cup finals against Liverpool. It was also the campaign when he scored the club's only European hat-trick in a UEFA Cup Winners' Cup 5-1 victory over Castilla.

It was one of three trebles he scored in claret and blue, but they were eclipsed by two four-goal hauls in 1981. The first came in the 5-1 thrashing of Grimsby Town. Then, early into the Hammers' Division One return, Cross put in a memorable performance at White Hart Lane, scoring all four against Tottenham Hotspur.

CROSS

He signed off with a goal against Wolverhampton Wanderers in the last match of the season, his final game for the club, moving to Manchester City that summer.

Cross had developed as a youth at his local club Rochdale and ended his playing career with Aris Limassol in Cyprus, before holding a number of different coaching positions.

FULL NAME:
Brian Dear

POSITION:
Forward

DATE OF BIRTH:
18 September 1943

PLACE OF BIRTH:
West Ham

WEST HAM UNITED DEBUT:
29 August 1962

APPEARANCES:
85

GOALS:
39

A record-breaking five-goal haul in 1965 showed that Brian Dear was up to the task of leading the line for West Ham United when needed.

A stocky, powerful front-man, he made his Irons debut on the wing as a raw teenager in a goalless draw at Wolverhampton Wanderers. He retained his place for the next game, but then did not play again until right at the end of the season. It was as a left-winger, as the 1962/63 campaign was wrapped up with the 6-1 thrashing of relegated Manchester City. Unable to force his way past more established names, Dear remained a reserve for large periods.

When his first prolonged run in the side came, Dear really produced the goods. In 15 consecutive starts at the end of 1964/65, he netted 14 goals and greatly contributed to the Hammers' first senior European trophy.

Dear was part of the victorious Hammers' UEFA Cup Winners' Cup-winning side, beating TSV 1860 Munich 2-0 at Wembley. His goals in the cup-run were instrumental in reaching the final, scoring four, including one in the semi-final first-leg against Real Zaragoza.

A little over a month before the Wembley showpiece, Dear had taken the plaudits, having scored five goals in twenty minutes in the demolition of West Bromwich Albion. Scoring just before half-time, he nabbed four more after the break, setting an English record for the quickest time in which the feat had been achieved.

DEAR

His other stint as a regular was for the best part of the 1967/68 season. He was again utilised as a wide-man, his bustling style and wicked shot regularly bringing goals from the wing, including a hat-trick against Leicester City during a burst of seven goals in four matches.

After a loan spell with Brighton & Hove Albion, a move to Fulham and then a short stint at Millwall, Dear made a short-lived return to the Boleyn Ground, playing four games during the 1970/71 season.

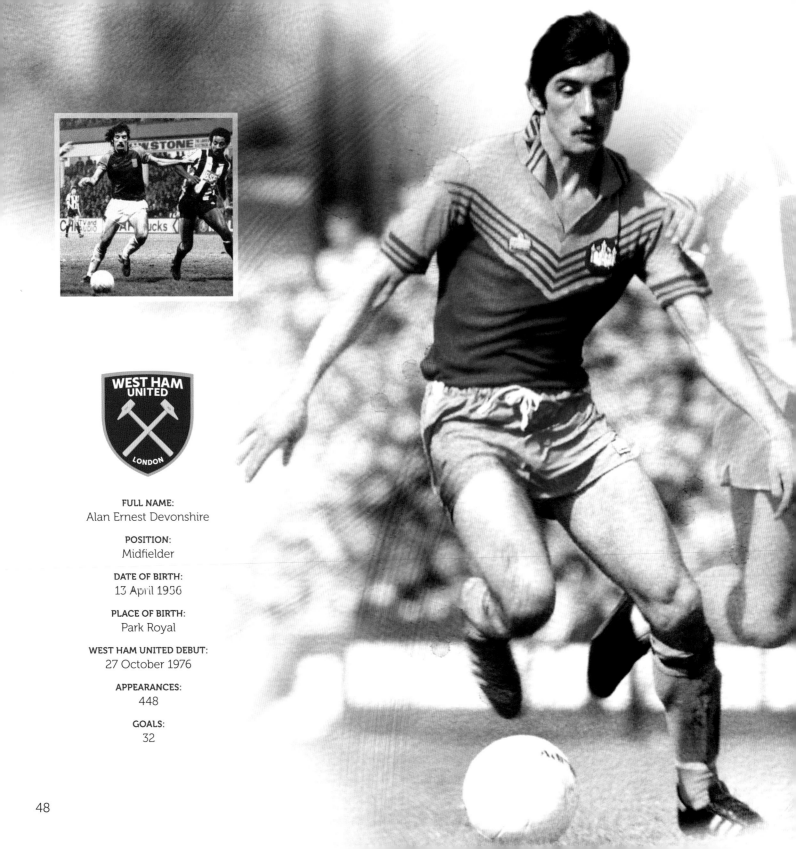

FULL NAME:
Alan Ernest Devonshire

POSITION:
Midfielder

DATE OF BIRTH:
13 April 1956

PLACE OF BIRTH:
Park Royal

WEST HAM UNITED DEBUT:
27 October 1976

APPEARANCES:
448

GOALS:
32

He may have been so down-to-earth that he would sometimes travel to games on the London Underground, but there was nothing understated about Alan Devonshire's performances on the pitch.

Dev was a slight figure, but he was deceptively tough and his direct style made him a firm favourite on the Boleyn Ground terraces. His size meant that professional clubs overlooked him as a youngster and it was only while playing non-league football that he was picked up by West Ham United, aged 20.

The nominal £5,000 fee paid to Southall proved to be a snip. After turning professional, Devonshire quickly showed he had what it took, despite playing in a struggling side. The Hammers lost four of his first five games, although the one exception was a thrilling 5-3 win against rivals Tottenham Hotspur.

With Devonshire's energy revitalising the team, a late-season rally brought about a seven-game unbeaten run that staved off relegation, for a season at least. West Ham were relegated at the end of 1977/78, but they opened the following campaign in Division Two with two victories, a 5-2 win at home to Notts County and a 3-0 triumph at St James' Park against the Magpies - Devonshire being on the score sheet on both occasions.

Voted Hammer of the Year at the end of the season, Devonshire also scored in comfortable victories over Preston North End, Luton Town and again Newcastle United as the Irons recovered from the shock of dropping down a division.

DEVONSHIRE

The club fell just short of promotion, but the following campaign they pulled off one of their greatest achievements, with Dev playing a huge part. A brilliant solo goal against Everton at Elland Road helped take West Ham to the 1980 FA Cup final, where Trevor Brooking's winner against the Gunners came as a result of one of his typically purposeful runs down the wing.

Ten days after winning the FA Cup, Devonshire was back at Wembley making his England debut against Northern Ireland and after the summer, he helped his club side on their march to the Division Two title.

Five goals in four league games, all wins, in early 1981, saw Devonshire help the Irons cement their place at the top of the table and he was back at the national stadium again for the League Cup final.

Once back in the top flight, Devonshire continued his good form and returned to the England side, but a serious knee injury sustained in a FA Cup tie against Wigan Athletic in early 1984 saw him miss over a year-and-a-half of football. An attempted comeback led to two further cup appearances in March 1985, but Devonshire did not fully recover until the start of the 1985/86 campaign. His return coincided with the club's highest-ever finish.

Another major injury on the opening day of the 1987/88 season led to another 13 months out of action, and Devonshire proved to be a big miss. He showed plenty of heart to make another comeback and despite those two big absences, he still became one of the club's highest appearance makers, before being given a free transfer by former teammate Billy Bonds in 1990.

In the summer of 1989, Devonshire had been given a testimonial against one of his father Les' old clubs, Crystal Palace - who ironically had released Alan as a youth.

DEVONSHIRE

His final Irons appearance came in the League Cup, the same competition he had debuted in 14 years earlier and in which he had scored a brace during the club's record 10-0 win over Bury.

A two-year spell at Watford followed before his playing career ended in 1992.

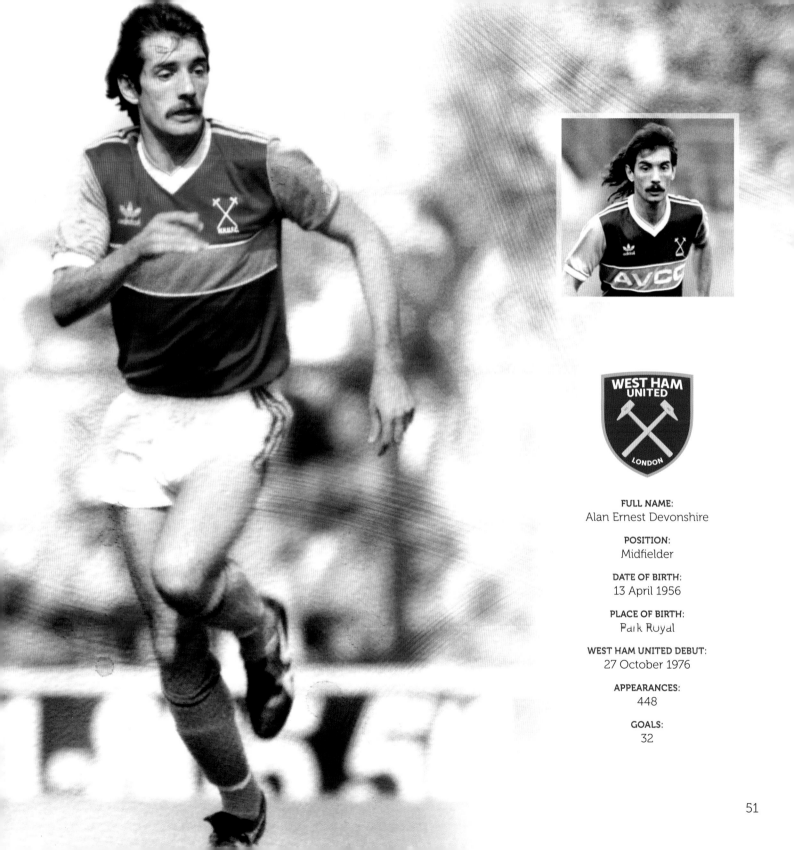

FULL NAME:
Alan Ernest Devonshire

POSITION:
Midfielder

DATE OF BIRTH:
13 April 1956

PLACE OF BIRTH:
Park Royal

WEST HAM UNITED DEBUT:
27 October 1976

APPEARANCES:
448

GOALS:
32

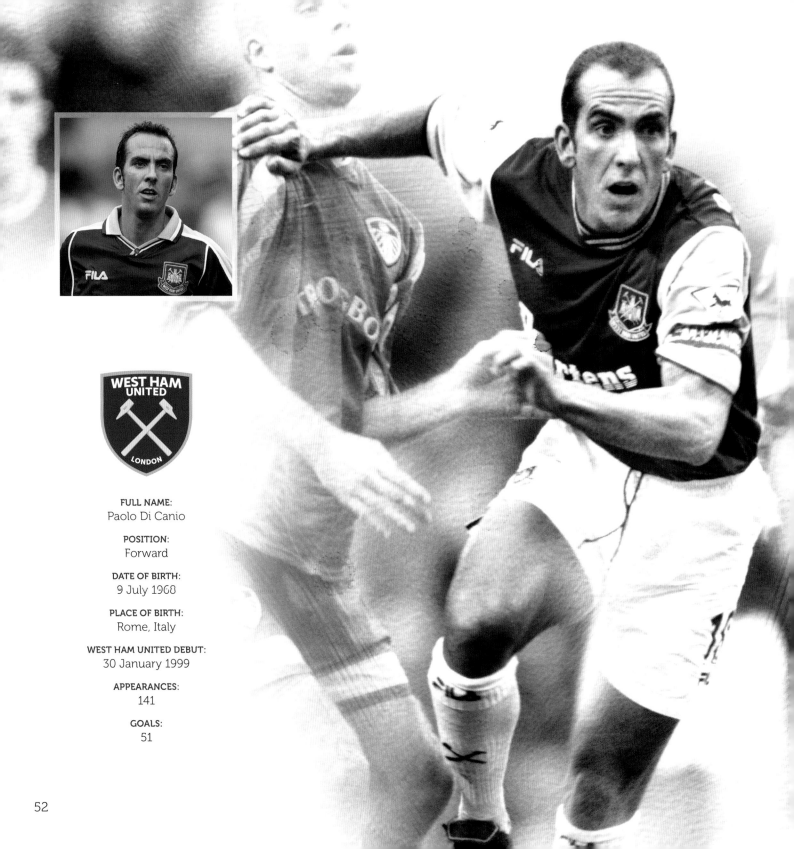

FULL NAME:
Paolo Di Canio

POSITION:
Forward

DATE OF BIRTH:
9 July 1968

PLACE OF BIRTH:
Rome, Italy

WEST HAM UNITED DEBUT:
30 January 1999

APPEARANCES:
141

GOALS:
51

There was never a dull moment in Paolo Di Canio's career, but after arriving at the Boleyn Ground with a controversial reputation, he consistently produced.

The Italian maestro fought hard for his chance to play the beautiful game. He admitted to being overweight as a child, but was immensely driven and became hugely dedicated to training and clean living.

A Lazio fan, Di Canio signed for the club he adored at the age of 17. A loan at cash-strapped Ternana provided good grounding and after Lazio's promotion back into Serie A in 1988, he quickly became a regular back at his hometown club. In the first derby game with Roma that season, Di Canio grabbed the winner ...and the adulation of the fans.

A transfer to Italian giants Juventus followed, with Di Canio appearing in both legs of the 1993 UEFA Cup final as the Old Lady crushed Borussia Dortmund 6-1 on aggregate. After a season at Napoli, another deal took him to AC Milan where he helped the Rossoneri beat his old club Juve to the 1995/96 Scudetto, before a move to the British Isles and Celtic.

He became headline news and was handed the PFA Scotland Players' Player of the Year award for 1996/97, but was soon on his travels again when David Pleat signed him for Sheffield Wednesday. Di Canio quickly adapted to the pace of the Premier League and became a popular figure, with supporters naming him Player of the Year, as the club just avoided relegation.

Di Canio's time in Yorkshire hit the buffers spectacularly the following season though, with his infamous moment-of-madness against Arsenal

DI CANIO

when he pushed referee Paul Alcock, resulting in an eleven-game ban, meaning he never played for the Owls again.

Harry Redknapp stepped in and offered Di Canio a fresh start, and, determined to repay the faith shown, he produced a series of inspired displays. A passionate man and player, his style matched his colourful character - often doing the unexpected.

It soon became clear that West Ham United, as a club, suited Paolo Di Canio perfectly. His arm now boasts a Hammers tattoo, the love shown to him from the Boleyn faithful truly reciprocated.

With their new talisman, West Ham finished the 1998/99 Premiership campaign in fifth place, and began the following season by winning the UEFA Intertoto Cup, Di Canio playing in both legs of the final against Metz. He ended the season as Hammer of the Year, also winning the coveted BBC Goal of the Season competition, with his unforgettable scissor-kick in the 2-1 win against Wimbledon.

The following season, his great act of sportsmanship against Everton, not only earned him a standing ovation from the Goodison faithful, but the FIFA Fair Play Award too. In the dying minutes of the game with the score poised at 1-1, Di Canio caught the ball, stopping play with the goal at his mercy, to allow goalkeeper Paul Gerrard to receive treatment.

The charismatic Di Canio's time at the Boleyn Ground was full of highlights, from appearing in an Imperial Leather advert to knocking Manchester United out of the FA Cup at Old Trafford with an ice-cold finish. Di Canio found himself clean through and as Barthez froze, hand aloft appealing for offside, the Italian calmly slotted home the winning goal with the outside of his foot.

Coolness personified, he converted eleven penalties for the Hammers and missed only a handful of games in his final season with West Ham, scoring in both games as the Irons completed the double over Chelsea

DI CANIO

in 2002/03. The victories were in vain however, as the club was relegated and Di Canio was sold to Charlton Athletic.

After a year at the Valley he made an emotional return to Italy, but returned to England for his first managerial appointment at Swindon Town, and later with Sunderland.

Brilliant, passionate, controversial, Di Canio often divided opinion, but at the Boleyn Ground he was simply adored.

FULL NAME:
Paolo Di Canio

POSITION:
Forward

DATE OF BIRTH:
9 July 1968

PLACE OF BIRTH:
Rome, Italy

WEST HAM UNITED DEBUT:
30 January 1999

APPEARANCES:
141

GOALS:
51

FULL NAME:
John Hart Dick

POSITION:
Forward

DATE OF BIRTH:
19 March 1930

PLACE OF BIRTH:
Govan, Scotland

WEST HAM UNITED DEBUT:
19 August 1953

APPEARANCES:
367

GOALS:
177

Thirteen was not unlucky for Johnny Dick - he scored his first goal for West Ham United in his thirteenth appearance, opening the floodgates.

Spotted playing non-league football while completing National Service, he joined the Hammers before the start of the 1953/54 campaign and after breaking his duck against Derby County, he never went as many games without scoring again.

He bagged a hat-trick two games later as the Irons eased past Bury 5-0 and before the end of the season, played for the Scotland B team, coming up against teammate Harry Hooper in a 1-1 draw against England B. England were also the opponents in 1959, when Dick became the first Hammer to play for the Scottish senior side. By that point, he was a Division One player and it was no surprise when he scored four goals in West Ham's first three games back in the top flight.

Dick lead the line well and after teaming up with Vic Keeble, the partnership helped the Hammers clinch the 1957/58 Division Two title. He was top of the scoring charts in the promotion season, as he was on five other occasions, notching four goals in one game, as Rotherham United were thrashed 8-0. It was not the only time he hit a hot streak though, nor was that his only winners' medal.

Over November and December 1954, he scored seven goals in six games, five in two in early 1955 and between October 1957 and January 1958, he had a run of 15 strikes from 16 appearances.

DICK

A 1956 Southern Floodlight Cup and 1959 Essex Professional Cup winner, he netted in derby wins against Tottenham Hotspur on Christmas Day and Boxing Day 1958 and in another local double, during 1959/60, against Chelsea. These, and plenty of others, put Dick joint-third on the all-time scorers list at West Ham.

He moved to Brentford in 1962, spending three seasons at Griffin Park, later returning to the Boleyn Ground to coach the juniors.

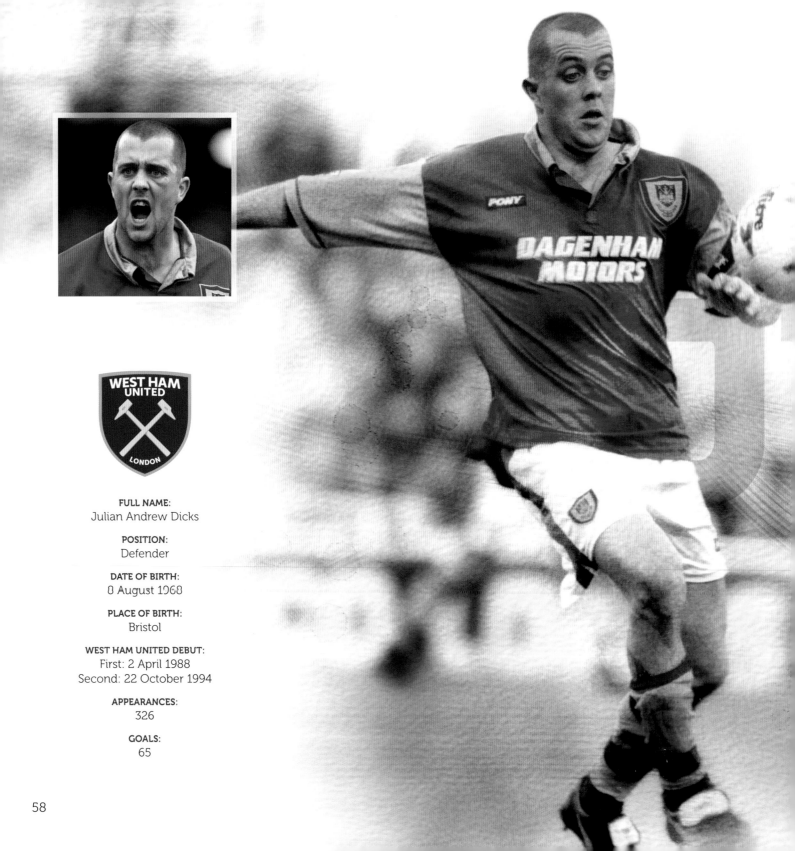

FULL NAME:
Julian Andrew Dicks

POSITION:
Defender

DATE OF BIRTH:
8 August 1968

PLACE OF BIRTH:
Bristol

WEST HAM UNITED DEBUT:
First: 2 April 1988
Second: 22 October 1994

APPEARANCES:
326

GOALS:
65

Julian Dicks' Benefit Match in August 2000 brought the curtain down on the career of one of West Ham United's most popular players ever, and fittingly for such a combative player, no quarter was given.

Spanish visitors Athletico Bilbao ensured the game had a competitive edge and shortly before half time, a mass brawl between the two sides lead to certain players having to be taken off for their own good. At that point, Dicks was not even on the pitch, but throughout his career he showed time and time again that he was not afraid of the physical side of the game.

His reputation to outsiders, as nothing more than a hardman, does not do Dicks justice. He was a dependable and highly committed full-back with a sweet left foot, capable of some quality long-range passing and the ability to take a mean free-kick or penalty.

There were of course, moments of ill-discipline, but if anything, his exuberance shown over two spells as a Hammer, only adds to Dicks' cult-hero status.

Dicks started out at Birmingham City and played under another West Ham full-back, John Bond, during his time at St Andrew's. He moved to London towards the end of the 1987/88 season, just as the club embarked on a period of mixed fortunes.

He featured in consecutive League Cup semi-finals and the club were promoted as Division Two runners-up twice in three seasons,

DICKS

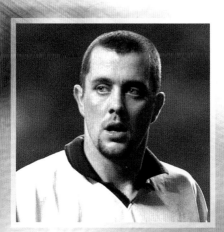

although he had to sit out the majority of the first success in 1990/91 due to an injury first picked up while playing in his hometown, against Bristol City.

His return to fitness came half-way through the following campaign, but Dicks could do little to stop the slump and the Irons were down again.

An integral part of the team that made an immediate return to the top flight in 1992/93, Dicks was sold to Liverpool following a poor start to the Hammers' first season in the Premiership.

His Anfield move allowed West Ham to remould their squad and pull away from danger. Dicks meanwhile, initially thrived on Merseyside under Graeme Souness, but when the Scot was replaced by Roy Evans it opened the door for the 'Terminator' to be back.

Dicks' second spell was spent entirely in the top division, although they did brush with relegation in the first season after his return. He was at his best when the going got tough and having lead the charge to survival, he ended up being named Hammer of the Year the following campaign - his selection helped by a cameo performance between the sticks at Everton following Ludek Miklosko's dismissal.

He also had an eye for goal. He was top scorer outright in 1989/90 and as well as tying with Paul Kitson for the honour in 1996/97, Dicks was again named Hammer of the Year.

It was the fourth occasion he had taken the award, having won it twice in the early 1990s, but his reign came to an end with him sitting out the whole of the 1997/98 season with a knee problem. A return to the first team followed, but his role was limited and Dicks retired from professional football in 1999, having twice been named in the PFA Team of the Year for Division Two and represented his country at both U21 and B levels.

DICKS

He did make a brief return to non-league football in 2001 and only days after signing for Canvey Island, he was part of the side that knocked Wigan Athletic out of the FA Cup, beating them 1-0 in the first round.

After several non-league management appointments, he took charge of West Ham United Ladies in 2014, before becoming part of Slaven Bilic's backroom staff in June 2015.

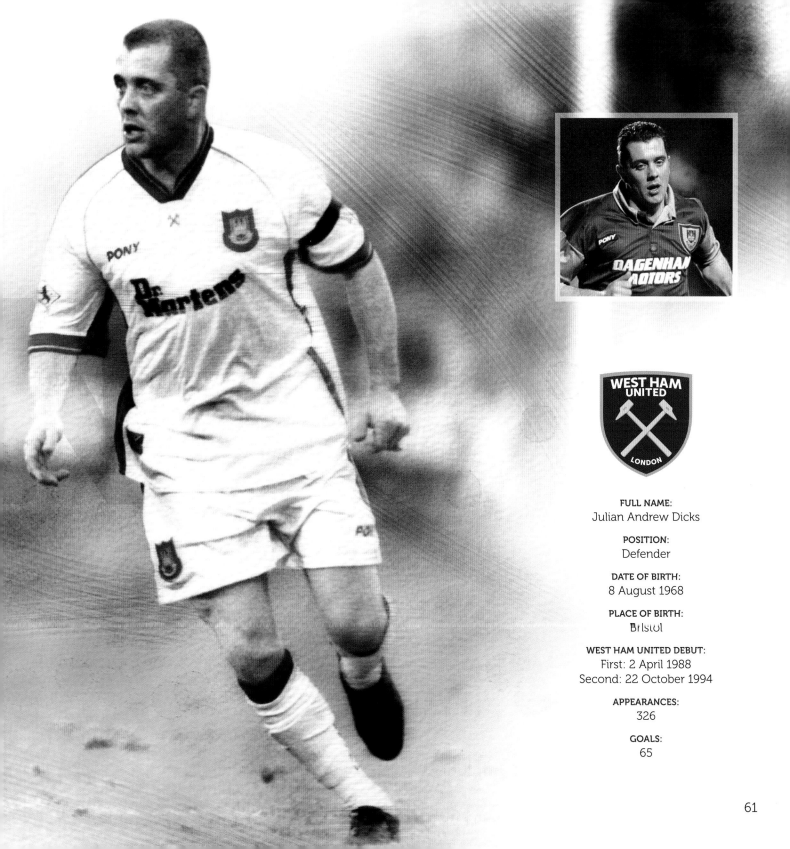

WEST HAM UNITED
LONDON

FULL NAME:
Julian Andrew Dicks

POSITION:
Defender

DATE OF BIRTH:
8 August 1968

PLACE OF BIRTH:
Bristol

WEST HAM UNITED DEBUT:
First: 2 April 1988
Second: 22 October 1994

APPEARANCES:
326

GOALS:
65

61

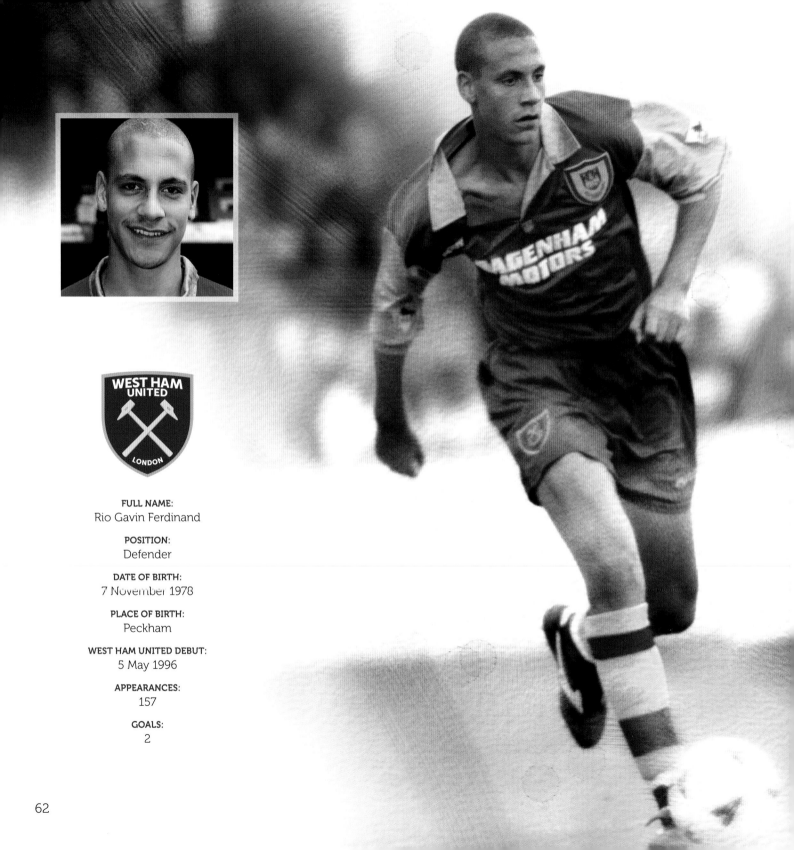

FULL NAME:
Rio Gavin Ferdinand

POSITION:
Defender

DATE OF BIRTH:
7 November 1978

PLACE OF BIRTH:
Peckham

WEST HAM UNITED DEBUT:
5 May 1996

APPEARANCES:
157

GOALS:
2

In Rio Ferdinand, the Academy of Football produced one of the greatest centre-backs of recent times. His transfers to Leeds United and Manchester United twice made him the world's most expensive defender.

He spent two seasons at Elland Road, before becoming a Red Devil in 2002. At Old Trafford he was hugely successful. As well as winning multiple domestic titles, Ferdinand captained Manchester United in the 2008 UEFA Champions League final victory over Chelsea. He also skippered the side to victory over Ecuadorians, LDU Quito in the FIFA Club World Cup final later that same year.

None of that may have been possible however, had it not been for Ferdinand's West Ham United schooling. He trained with several clubs before opting for the Hammers, who had been alerted to his talents by Frank Lampard Senior. Along with Frank Junior, Ferdinand was part of an exciting crop of youngsters coming through under the revered Tony Carr and made his senior debut days after appearing in the FA Youth Cup final.

Ferdinand was an all-round defender, graceful on the pitch and extremely comfortable with the ball at his feet. In late 1996, he gained experience on loan at Bournemouth and after enjoying an extended run, once back at the Boleyn, he ended the season as Young Hammer of the Year. The following season he was voted Hammer of the Year outright, as the club were comfortable top-half finishers during Ferdinand's three full seasons as a regular.

FERDINAND

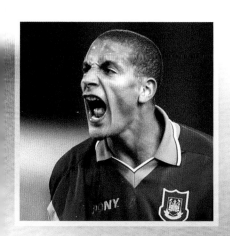

Having previously captained England U18s, he also gained the first of his 81 international caps while at the Boleyn Ground. Shortly after his 19th birthday, he came on as a first-half substitute for injured Gareth Southgate, in the 2-0 friendly victory over Cameroon .

Ferdinand's career eventually came full circle, retiring in 2015 after a season with Queens Park Rangers, back in the city he had grown up in.

A familiar face to many through his work as a television pundit and columnist, Tony Gale often speaks passionately in the media about the club he served so well for almost ten years.

A well-liked figure in the changing room, Gale now shows all that charm and ease in front of the cameras off the pitch having previously enjoyed a sterling career on it. Gale started his career in West London at Fulham and as a youngster was in the same squad as Bobby Moore, who at that point was at the other end of his career.

His senior debut came in the Anglo-Scottish Cup at Orient, aged just 16. The side lost, but within two years, Gale was named captain and became a stand-out performer at Craven Cottage. He was instrumental in Fulham's 1981/82 promotion and was selected for the Division Three PFA Team of the Year.

Fulham finished third in the final promotion berth, a point ahead of Lincoln City and only two points behind champions Burnley. They went extremely close to a second successive promotion in 1982/83, missing out by a single point after another tight campaign.

Gale comfortably managed the step up in class, again being named in the PFA Team of the Year, but with the side managing only a mid-table finish the following campaign, he was snapped up by West Ham United.

GALE

Once more, Gale made the jump in standard look easy after making his Hammers debut for John Lyall in a goalless draw with Ipswich Town in the 1984/85 season opener. Also playing that day was new teammate Paul Goddard, who had scored for England U21s when Gale played for his country in 1982. The game was in Warsaw and Goddard's early goal set up a 2-1 win over Poland.

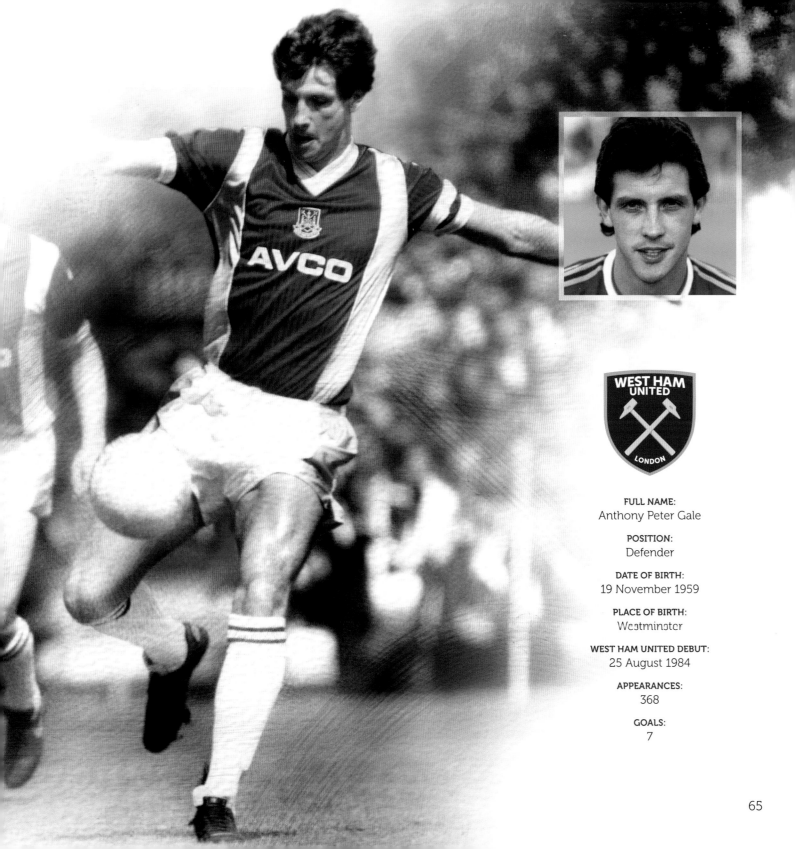

FULL NAME:
Anthony Peter Gale

POSITION:
Defender

DATE OF BIRTH:
19 November 1959

PLACE OF BIRTH:
Westminster

WEST HAM UNITED DEBUT:
25 August 1984

APPEARANCES:
368

GOALS:
7

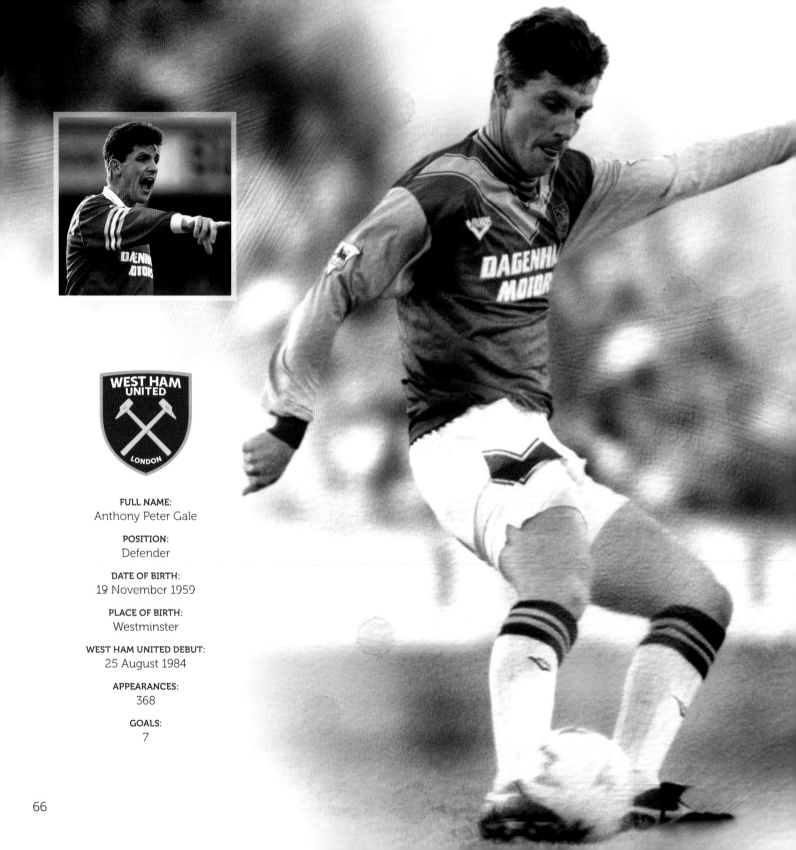

FULL NAME:
Anthony Peter Gale

POSITION:
Defender

DATE OF BIRTH:
19 November 1959

PLACE OF BIRTH:
Westminster

WEST HAM UNITED DEBUT:
25 August 1984

APPEARANCES:
368

GOALS:
7

Supporters still talk ruefully about Gale's infamous dismissal in the 1991 FA Cup semi-final against Nottingham Forest. He was controversially sent off after less than half-an-hour, having been deemed to have fouled Cary Crosby, but there were plenty of good times too.

He showed guile in the centre of defence and was such an accomplished and intelligent player, he could fill a gap in midfield when required. Gale's near-post flick-ons from corners were a well-used tactic too and he was a key part of the great Hammers team of 1985/86. He helped the 'Boys of 86' rack up nine consecutive league wins and towards the end of the season, thump Newcastle United 8-1, in the first of four home wins on the trot, which gave the Irons a chance of winning the league.

Gale was ever-present as the club achieved their highest-ever third place finish, winning 26 of their 42 games and finishing just four points behind double-winners Liverpool.

The following season started with a victory over Coventry City, Gale scoring his first goal, two days short of the second anniversary of his debut. Arguably his best strike was a pearler against Liverpool en-route to the first of two League Cup semi-finals, and Gale had a hand in two promotion successes too, in 1991 and 1993.

His Irons career ended in 1994 with a testimonial against a Republic of Ireland XI, before adding a bit of know-how to Blackburn Rovers'

GALE

squad and helping them lift the 1994/95 Premier League title.

After a season at Crystal Palace, Gale later played under former teammate Alan Devonshire at Maidenhead United and his non-league involvement continued at Walton Casuals, whom he joined in 2002, first as Director of Football and later Chairman.

Paul Goddard was a busy striker, full of running with plenty of talent to go with his work rate. He was a record club buy when he joined West Ham United from Queens Park Rangers in 1980.

He scored his first goal for the club in the League Cup second round at Burnley and also netted in the League Cup final replay against Liverpool later the same season. Liverpool won the trophy, but Goddard had been bought primarily to help win promotion and the Hammers achieved their goal in style, with their new striker grabbing 17 league goals on the way to the Division Two title.

One of eight Hammers included in the PFA Team of the Year, Goddard linked up with David Cross to devastating effect - the side were the division's highest scorers and finished with a goal difference of plus 50.

A hat-trick during the run-in against former club QPR, was followed early on into West Ham's top-flight return with another, Goddard and teammates showing they could handle the top flight with a 4-2 win over Southampton.

His instinctive partnership with Cross continued and at the end of the campaign, Goddard made his England debut, scoring again in a 1-1 draw in Iceland. He followed that by finishing the following 1982/83 season as the Irons' joint-top marksman with Francois Van der Elst.

GODDARD

Desperately unlucky with injuries, two of the next three campaigns were virtual write-offs. Supporters were sorry to see him leave in 1986, his move north to Newcastle United making him the club's record sale at the time.

A teammate of Glenn Roeder while in the North East, Goddard returned to the Boleyn Ground 15 years later to work as part of Roeder's back-room staff.

FULL NAME:
Paul Goddard

POSITION:
Forward

DATE OF BIRTH:
12 October 1959

PLACE OF BIRTH:
Harlington

WEST HAM UNITED DEBUT:
16 August 1980

APPEARANCES:
213

GOALS:
71

WEST HAM UNITED LONDON

FULL NAME:
Ernest Gregory

POSITION:
Goalkeeper

DATE OF BIRTH:
10 November 1921

PLACE OF BIRTH:
Stratford

WEST HAM UNITED DEBUT:
28 December 1946

APPEARANCES:
422*

*does not include war-time competitions

Club stalwart Ernie Gregory went ten years between joining the ground staff and finally making his Football League bow, but that was only the beginning of his amazing association with West Ham United.

Gregory cut his teeth as an amateur, playing between the sticks for Leytonstone while still working at the Boleyn Ground, before the outbreak of World War Two. He served in the forces and featured for the club in war-time competitions, but after hostilities ended and the Football League resumed, Gregory was down the pecking order.

When he was given his debut in 1946, it proved to be a comfortable victory over Plymouth Argyle. After an extended run in the side at the end of the season, Gregory made the goalkeepers' jersey his own and was ever-present for the following 1947/48 campaign.

The Hammers were a second tier side for the majority of Gregory's playing career, but with him in the eleven, they shared the Essex Professional Cup in 1955, drawing 3-3 with Southend United and won the Southern Floodlight Cup in 1956, beating Aldershot 2-1.

Eventually promoted back to the top flight as Division Two champions in 1957/58, Gregory helped the side hold their nerve to win the title by a point. He remained first choice as the club firmly established themselves back in Division One.

There was over a year between his final game and a testimonial match in 1960, against Costa Rican side Liga Deportiva Alajeulense, and by

GREGORY

then he was working behind the scenes.

A coach and club official, Gregory was an integral part of the Hammers' fabric during many successful eras. Even after his formal retirement in 1987, he was known to still help out with some of the younger goalkeepers, passing on tips from a distinguished career that included an England B cap in 1952.

FULL NAME:
John Hartson

POSITION:
Forward

DATE OF BIRTH:
5 April 1975

PLACE OF BIRTH:
Swansea

WEST HAM UNITED DEBUT:
15 February 1997

APPEARANCES:
73

GOALS:
33

Having started his career at Luton Town, Hartson arrived at West Ham United as a club-record signing from Arsenal. He immediately struck up an instinctive partnership with fellow new-boy Paul Kitson, that spearheaded the Hammers' rise out of the relegation zone.

Braces against Coventry and Sheffield Wednesday went a long way to ensuring top-flight football at the Boleyn, the Ground where he had scored the only goal of the game for the Gunners a year before switching clubs. He had also scored for Arsenal in the 1995 UEFA Cup Winners' Cup final loss to Real Zaragoza.

Hartson was a powerful frontman and hard to shake off the ball, but while he enjoyed the physical side of the game, he had some finesse too. His first touch was strong and while with the Irons, he scored the first of his 14 senior international goals, beating Scotland 1-0 in a friendly. He went on to win a total of 51 caps for Wales.

Early the following season, between August and December 1997, Hartson was on fire. The striker netted 17 goals in just 20 games, not only helping his side to derby victories over Tottenham Hotspur and Wimbledon, but reaching the League Cup quarter-finals along the way. He finished the campaign as the Irons' top scorer by some distance with 15 in the Premier League and 24 in all competitions.

He made a big-money move to Wimbledon in early 1999 and following a short spell at Coventry City, he journeyed north of the

HARTSON

border, enjoying five highly-successful seasons at Celtic. At Celtic Park, he won three league titles and three cup competitions, as well as ending 2004/05 as the Scottish Premier League's top scorer and the Scottish Football Writers' Association Player of the Year.

After two years at West Bromwich Albion, which included a loan spell at Norwich City, Hartson retired from the game he loved in 2008.

WEST HAM UNITED
LONDON

FULL NAME:
Patrick George Holland

POSITION:
Midfielder

DATE OF BIRTH:
13 September 1950

PLACE OF BIRTH:
Poplar

WEST HAM UNITED DEBUT:
21 April 1969

APPEARANCES:
304

GOALS:
32

Local boy Pat Holland took five seasons to nail down a starting spot in the West Ham United first team, but his breakthrough coincided with the club's best finish in years.

1972/73 saw the Hammers finish sixth in Division One, a position the club had not achieved since they had returned to the top flight in 1958/59. Holland had waited patiently for his chance to shine, but once established, he became a vital cog on the right hand side of midfield.

After graduating through the youth ranks, he made his senior debut in the penultimate game of the 1968/69 campaign. He did not feature again for nine months though and despite scoring the only goal of the game in a March 1970 win against Liverpool, he spent large periods out of the picture and did not become a regular until 1972.

Still learning his trade during the hiatus, in 1971, Holland went on loan to the south coast to play for the club then known as Bournemouth and Boscombe Athletic Football Club. Playing in Division Three, he worked under former Irons full-back John Bond and played alongside future West Ham teammate Ted MacDougall.

Having convinced Ron Greenwood, he was good enough to hold down a regular place in the side, 1972/73 saw Holland playing week in, week out for the Hammers. Hard working and often a player that liked to keep things simple, he grabbed the only goal of the game, in a battling FA Cup third round win at Port Vale early into the new year.

HOLLAND

He could also show an unexpected turn of pace and go on a mazy dribble when things opened up. That was the case a year later in 1974, when he scored a wonderful goal against Hereford United in the same competition.

Holland's slalom-run finish was memorable, even if Hammers fans prefer to forget the resulting replay defeat against the giant-killing Bulls.

FULL NAME:
Patrick George Holland

POSITION:
Midfielder

DATE OF BIRTH:
13 September 1950

PLACE OF BIRTH:
Poplar

WEST HAM UNITED DEBUT:
21 April 1969

APPEARANCES:
304

GOALS:
32

West Ham's next stab at the FA Cup was infinitely more successful however, and Holland had a major hand in bringing the FA Cup back to the Boleyn Ground.

He netted the decider in the fourth round replay at Swindon Town and was again on target in the next tie against Queens Park Rangers, before playing in the 2-0 FA Cup Final victory against Fulham that secured European qualification for the following season.

Holland's goal in the 1976 UEFA Cup Winners' Cup final defeat to Anderlecht was one of the few occasions when his strike proved to be in vain. The majority of his goals made a difference. Over the years, the Hammers only lost five matches in which Holland notched.

A year after defeat in Europe, Holland spent an intriguing couple of months playing for Team Hawaii in the North American Soccer League. The league was headed up by former Hammer Phil Woosnam, but Hawaii were unable to get past the regular season stage.

He was not done with the Boleyn Ground yet, and while relegation in 1978 meant Holland was playing in the second tier for the first time, the side were well on the way to promotion in 1980/81, thanks, in part, to his winners against Sheffield Wednesday and Orient.

Out injured for the 1980 FA Cup win the season earlier, Holland was forced to hang up his boots in January 1981. In scoring another vital goal in a 1-1 draw with Notts County, he injured his knee colliding with the 'keeper and his career came to a close.

HOLLAND

Holland was a great servant to the club and a favourite on the terraces. He continued with the Hammers as a coach until 1984 and following a testimonial against Tottenham Hotspur, 'Patsy' went on to enjoy several more coaching positions in and around London.

On 30 July 1966, Geoff Hurst became the toast of the nation, but just four years earlier he looked more likely to be catching wickets than he did scoring a hat-trick in a FIFA World Cup final.

After making his football debut in a Southern Floodlight Cup match, Hurst did not feature again for the West Ham United first team until helping them win the Essex Professional Cup final nine months later. Even after that he was only used sporadically, but after moving into midfield he started to get regular games.

The end of the 1962/63 campaign took the club to the United States of America for the International Soccer League. After finishing the competition as top scorer, including grabbing the winning goal in the Play-Off final against Gornik Zabrze of Poland, it became crystal clear that Hurst's strength lay in the forward-line.

It helped spark a golden age for the club and player alike. An ever-present throughout the run, Hurst's contribution was instrumental in the Hammers lifting the 1964 FA Cup, scoring seven goals along the way including one in the final as Preston North End were defeated 3-2.

Choosing to concentrate on football, Hurst stopped playing for Essex Cricket Club as a wicket-keeper, but success continued on the football pitch. The club won the UEFA Cup Winners' Cup in 1965 with Hurst once more playing in every game of the competition, and for the third season in a row, 1966 ended with a showpiece occasion at Wembley Stadium.

HURST

Hurst had only made his England debut five months earlier and did not even begin their World Cup campaign as a regular starter. In the team for the injured Jimmy Greaves, he secured the home nation's semi-final place, converting clubmate Martin Peters' cross to score the only goal of an ill-tempered game against Argentina.

He kept the number ten shirt for the 2-1 semi-final victory over Portugal and for the World Cup final - where his three goals in the 4-2 triumph over West Germany have become part of sporting folklore.

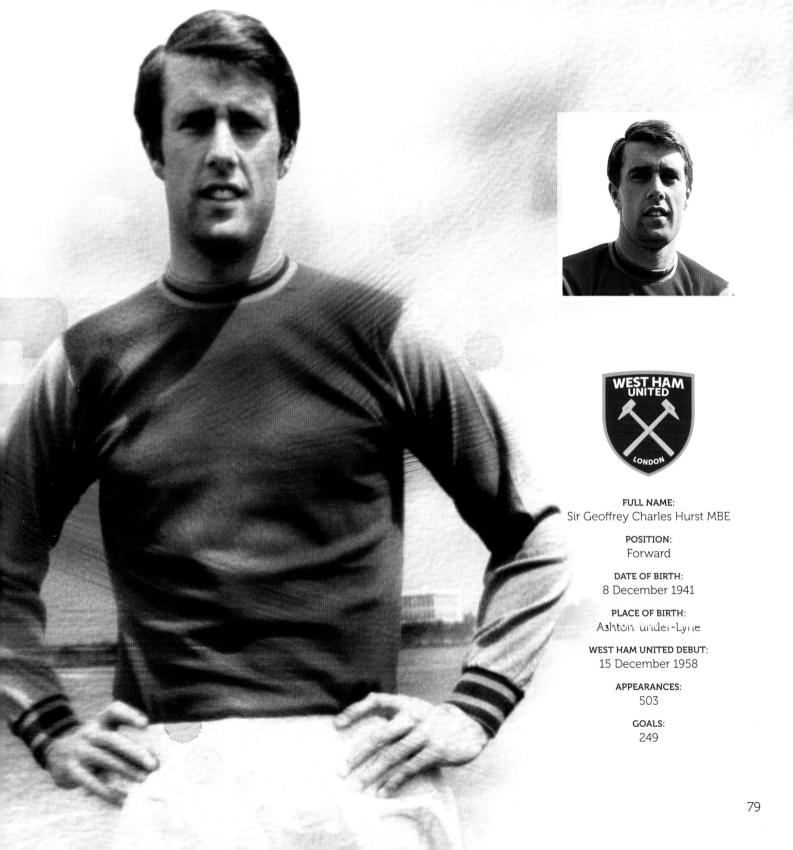

FULL NAME:
Sir Geoffrey Charles Hurst MBE

POSITION:
Forward

DATE OF BIRTH:
8 December 1941

PLACE OF BIRTH:
Ashton-under-Lyne

WEST HAM UNITED DEBUT:
15 December 1958

APPEARANCES:
503

GOALS:
249

79

Hurst had been named Hammer of the Year for the first time in 1966, having scored 40 goals for the club, three of which came in the two-legged League Cup semi-final win over Cardiff City.

His stock was high and the following 1966/67 season, he was voted Hammer of the Year for the second time. He scored four goals in a game on two occasions and then surpassed that when he became only the second man to score six goals in a single match for West Ham, almost 60 years after Vic Watson's double hat-trick against Leeds United

Hurst's six-goal haul came at Sunderland's expense in October 1968, and at the end of the 1968/69 campaign, he was again named Hammer of the Year. A very unselfish worker in general play, he came alive in the penalty area and could make the most of even half chances.

In October 1970, Hurst scored in a 2-2 draw with Tottenham Hotspur in front of a record Boleyn Ground league attendance. Crowds averaged over 30,000 for only the second time in Hammers history that season, but results did not reach the same heights and Hurst's three goals in the final four fixtures were desperately needed to maintain Division One status.

It meant that Hurst's time at the club was spent entirely in the top flight and he remains the Irons' top post Second World War scorer despite being sold to Stoke City in 1972.

HURST

There were moves to South Africa, the Republic of Ireland and America later, plus a managerial post in Kuwait, but it is in England where he is still held in the highest regard.

Awarded an MBE in 1975 and knighted in 1998, Hurst was inducted into the English Football Hall of Fame six years later and remains a true club and international great.

FULL NAME:
Sir Geoffrey Charles Hurst MBE

POSITION:
Forward

DATE OF BIRTH:
8 December 1941

PLACE OF BIRTH:
Ashton-under-Lyne

WEST HAM UNITED DEBUT:
15 December 1958

APPEARANCES:
503

GOALS:
249

West Ham United manager Ted Fenton knew exactly what he was getting when he bought Vic Keeble, and it did not take long to show everybody else either.

Keeble played under Fenton at Colchester United and following a successful 1949/50 season that saw them win the Southern Football League Cup and finish second in the table, the club were elected to the Football League. After moving to Newcastle United, Keeble again had a hand in success, playing in the 1955 FA Cup final win over Manchester City, two years before reuniting with Fenton at West Ham.

Keeble had an instant impact on the day of his Boleyn Ground arrival. He played in Dick Walker's testimonial and in front of a healthy 19,375 crowd, struck up an immediate relationship with John Dick. The pair both scored against Sparta Rotterdam and five days later, Keeble was again on target as the Hammers drew 1-1 with Doncaster Rovers on his competitive debut.

Plenty more followed, an early hat-trick against Stoke City pushed the Irons into Division Two's leading pack, before a brace in the 6-2 thumping of Swansea Town put them top of the table. Keeble was the final piece of the jigsaw and his added impetus helped turn the side from one that had finished eighth the previous season into title winners, with him again scoring as promotion was secured with a 3-1 victory at Middlesbrough.

Back in Division One the side quickly found their feet, Keeble scoring four in the 6-3 demolition of Blackburn Rovers. The club had a strong

KEEBLE

season, finishing in sixth place and 1959/60 started well too, but after beginning with five goals in seven games, a back injury sustained against Fulham took hold and Keeble was forced to retire from the game.

A devastating forward with a claret and blue goal-rate of virtually one every game and a half, Keeble later returned to the Southern League as club secretary at Chelmsford City.

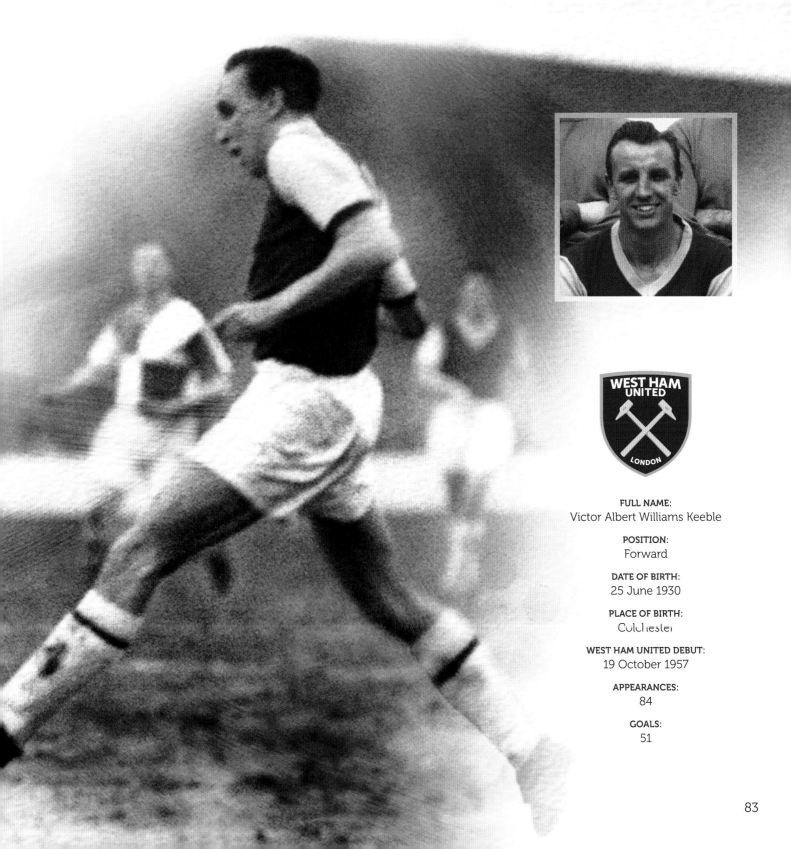

FULL NAME:
Victor Albert Williams Keeble

POSITION:
Forward

DATE OF BIRTH:
25 June 1930

PLACE OF BIRTH:
Colchester

WEST HAM UNITED DEBUT:
19 October 1957

APPEARANCES:
84

GOALS:
51

The modern-day Academy of Football helped bring through one of the country's most capped players ever, in the form of Frank Lampard Junior.

Lampard was still at West Ham United when he made his full international debut at Sunderland's Stadium of Light in October 1999. The winning goal in the 2-1 victory over Belgium that day was Lampard's cousin, Jamie Redknapp.

Despite Lampard's uncle, Harry Redknapp, being the Hammers' boss and his father, Frank Lampard Senior, being not only the assistant manager but also a former fans' favourite himself, Lampard Junior was his own man and a highly-driven performer.

By the time he appeared in the 1996 FA Youth Cup final for the Irons, Lampard had already made two substitute appearances for the first team and been on loan at Swansea City. Adopting a cautious approach, the Hammers eased him in gradually, before injury curtailed his 1996/97 season.

The following campaign proved to be Lampard's real breakthrough. Fit again, he scored his first goal for the club, to start the season with a win at Barnsley. Showing verve and the ability to make even the most difficult things look easy, many felt he was the complete midfielder. After two top-half Premiership finishes, Lampard was a scorer in the second leg of the UEFA Intertoto final success against Metz.

LAMPARD JNR

The following season, with both his father and uncle leaving the club, Lampard opted for a fresh start with Chelsea. At Stamford Bridge, he became one of the most celebrated stars of the Premier League era. The Pensioners' record goal scorer and a multiple trophy winner, Lampard also received the Ballon d'Or silver award in 2005.

Ten years later, he was awarded an OBE, shortly after ending a season with Manchester City. That summer, Lampard made his debut for New York City.

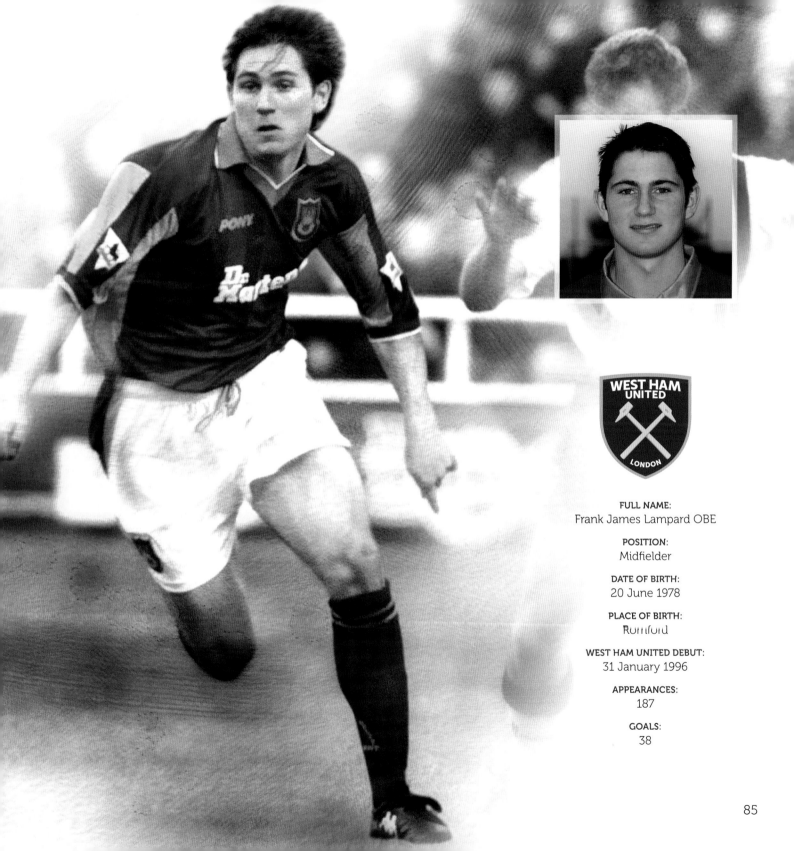

FULL NAME:
Frank James Lampard OBE

POSITION:
Midfielder

DATE OF BIRTH:
20 June 1978

PLACE OF BIRTH:
Romford

WEST HAM UNITED DEBUT:
31 January 1996

APPEARANCES:
187

GOALS:
38

85

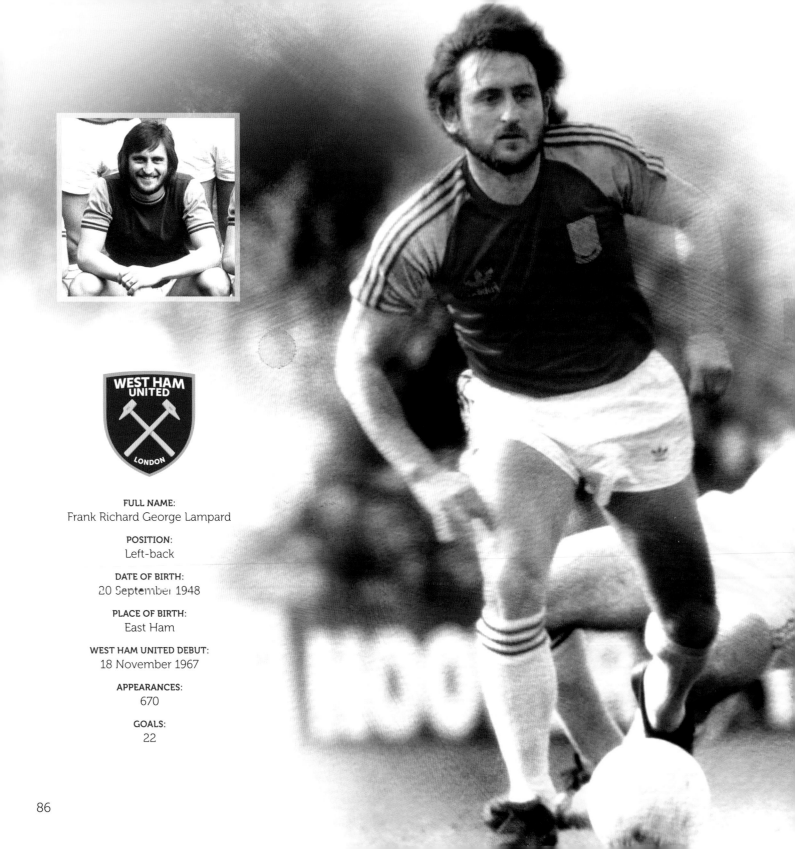

FULL NAME:
Frank Richard George Lampard

POSITION:
Left-back

DATE OF BIRTH:
20 September 1948

PLACE OF BIRTH:
East Ham

WEST HAM UNITED DEBUT:
18 November 1967

APPEARANCES:
670

GOALS:
22

The second highest appearance maker in West Ham United history, Frank Lampard Senior was a product of the club's youth system and after debuting against Manchester City at the Boleyn Ground in 1967, he quickly became a first-team regular.

His campaign was cut short however, after breaking a leg at Bramall Lane in the latter stages of an away win over Sheffield United. It was a year and three days before Lampard would play again, with City the opponents once more. Now in the team to stay, he proved a fantastic servant to the club, comfortable on the ball and always available for a pass, he remained first choice left-back for the next fifteen seasons.

Lampard was superb in both the 1975 and 1980 FA Cup glories. His goal against Southampton in the third round, set them on the way to Wembley for the first success, but perhaps his most enduring moment came in the 1980 semi-final replay against Everton at Elland Road. With only two minutes to go and a second replay imminent, Lampard arrived on cue, grabbing the winner with a full-length diving header, prompting his memorable victory dance around the corner flag.

In between the FA Cup triumphs, the club awarded Lampard a testimonial match, Fulham providing the opposition in 1976. He also picked up a losers' medal that same year, in the UEFA Cup Winners' Cup final 4-2 defeat by Anderlecht. A League Cup finalist in 1980/81, Lampard was also part of the formidable Hammers side that took the Division Two title by storm, adding another medal to go alongside his international caps.

LAMPARD SNR

Four England U23 appearances in 1972 led to the first of his two senior caps. A 1-1 draw against Yugoslavia at Wembley was followed eight years later with a friendly win in Australia.

After playing his last game for the Hammers against Liverpool in 1985, he spent his final season playing for a Southend United side managed by another West Ham legend, Bobby Moore. Lampard returned to the Boleyn Ground in 1994 and spent seven seasons as assistant-manager to brother-in-law, Harry Redknapp.

Andy Malcolm was the only league ever-present when West Ham United won Division Two in 1957/58. He was exactly the type of steely, dogged performer every successful side needs.

While the team's fortunes varied in the seasons prior, Malcolm's displays remained constant. Named the first-ever Hammer of the Year for the promotion season and an Essex Professional Cup winner in 1959, he clocked 110 consecutive league appearances between August 1957 and January 1960, missing only nine league matches in five seasons.

Local boy Malcolm had a strong pedigree when he signed professional forms in 1950. Two years before, he became the first Irons player to get an England youth call-up, representing his country in the inaugural International Youth Association Football Tournament - a forerunner to the UEFA European Under-19 Championship. West Ham staged two of the fixtures with hosts England winning the competition.

Having worked through the various Hammers A and Mid-Week sides, Malcolm proved his worth for the reserves, who in 1953/54 completed an unprecedented Football Combination league and cup double. He won a further representative honour in 1958, playing for the Football League in a draw against a Scottish League select team at Ibrox Stadium. Four years later he transferred to Chelsea but despite being named the Blues' new club captain, he departed for Queens Park Rangers after only one season.

MALCOLM

He later played in South Africa at both Port Elizabeth and Apollen FC. He came back to England and turned out for Brentwood Town in the Southern League during 1967/68, but after a spell in the pub trade emigrated and settled back in Port Elizabeth.

He remained in South Africa until his death on Boxing Day 2013, the same day the Hammers hosted Arsenal at the Boleyn Ground, where in 1960 Malcolm had scored his final goal for the club, when the same opposition were routed 6-0.

FULL NAME:
Andy Malcolm

POSITION:
Midfielder

DATE OF BIRTH:
4 May 1933

PLACE OF BIRTH:
Upton Park

WEST HAM UNITED DEBUT:
22 October 1953

APPEARANCES:
321

GOALS:
4

Alvin Martin enjoyed a magnificent career at the Boleyn Ground, but he could have easily been playing his football over in Shepherds Bush instead.

After turning down an apprenticeship at Everton upon leaving school, Martin came to London in 1974 and had a trial at Queens Park Rangers followed by one at West Ham United a day later. The Hammers liked what they saw and tied up the deal. After serving his time with the youth side and appearing for the club in the 1975 FA Youth Cup final, Martin signed professional terms two years later.

The senior side lifted the FA Cup that season, beating Fulham 2-0, and five years later they returned to Wembley with Martin now fully established in the side, having debuted for the first team during the 1977/78 relegation season.

Martin was thrust in at the deep end, coming on as a substitute in a damaging 4-1 loss to Aston Villa. The side were already in serious trouble and while a goal against Leeds United in his first start briefly lifted spirits, the Irons had given themselves too much to do and ultimately failed to beat the drop.

A return to Division Two meant young prospects like Martin were properly blooded and half-way through the season, the beginnings of an instinctive central-defensive pairing with Billy Bonds were there to see. Like Bonds, Martin was also rewarded with two separate testimonial games for his services over two decades with the club.

MARTIN

On both occasions, London rivals provided the opposition. Tottenham Hotspur were beaten 2-0 in 1988 and seven years later, a Chelsea XI took part in an entertaining 3-3 draw with several guest stars turning out. Chris Waddle, Steve McManaman and Jamie Redknapp all made appearances, along with Chelsea's manager Glenn Hoddle.

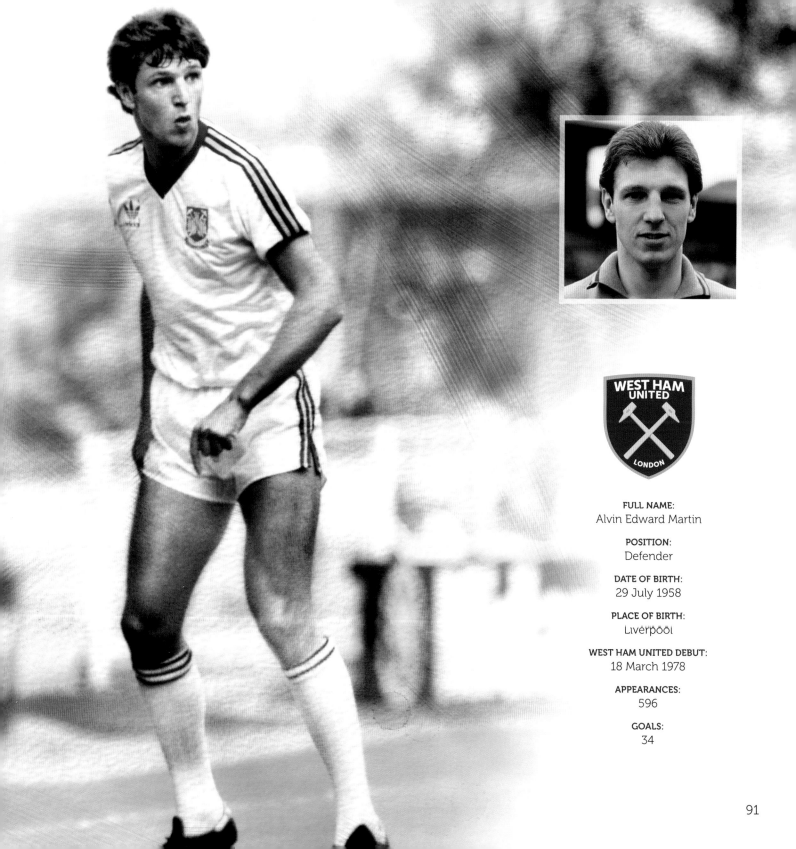

FULL NAME:
Alvin Edward Martin

POSITION:
Defender

DATE OF BIRTH:
29 July 1958

PLACE OF BIRTH:
Liverpool

WEST HAM UNITED DEBUT:
18 March 1978

APPEARANCES:
596

GOALS:
34

FULL NAME:
Alvin Edward Martin

POSITION:
Defender

DATE OF BIRTH:
29 July 1958

PLACE OF BIRTH:
Liverpool

WEST HAM UNITED DEBUT:
18 March 1978

APPEARANCES:
596

GOALS:
34

The Bonds-Martin unit went from strength to strength as the club marched to their 1980 FA Cup Wembley win, and while Martin missed the semi-final replay victory over Everton his Wembley place was never in doubt.

His cup winners' medal was accompanied by the Hammer of the Year award in 1980 and after securing promotion as Division Two Champions the following campaign, he was also included in the PFA Team of the Year.

1981 also saw Martin make his England debut against Brazil at Wembley. Back in the top flight and now an international, he was becoming one of the most proficient defenders in the country. Strong in the air and ultra organised, 'Stretch', as he was known due to the ease in which he tackled, was the backbone of the team. Hammer of the Year twice more in 1982 and 1983, he took over the captaincy from Bonds and embarked on another intuitive connection at the heart of the defence, dovetailing with Tony Gale as West Ham achieved their best-ever league finish.

Martin scored a memorable hat-trick against Newcastle United that season and ended it with a trip to Mexico for the 1986 FIFA World Cup, playing in England's Second Round victory over Paraguay. He had missed the 1982 tournament through injury and in the later stages of his career was beset with various spells on the treatment table - even his first testimonial in 1988 served as a comeback, having been out injured for six months.

MARTIN

When available though, Martin continued to produce the goods and even in his mid-thirties kept coming back for more. His know-how proved vital to those around him and it was apt that his final game came as the club celebrated its Centenary against Sporting Lisbon.

A huge figure in the history of West Ham United, his sons David and Joe were also on the books as youngsters and have since forged their own careers in the game.

A relative-unknown when John Lyall brought him to West Ham United, Frank McAvennie soon became the man of the moment and enjoyed his hero status with the Boleyn Ground faithful.

Scottish PFA Young Player of the Year in 1982, McAvennie started out playing Scottish Junior League football for Johnstone Burgh before turning professional in 1980, when he joined Paisley-based club, St Mirren.

He netted twice on his senior debut in the 4-3 defeat of Airdrieonians and continued to show himself as an exciting talent, but few could have predicted the impact McAvennie would have for the Hammers when he moved south.

Arriving before the start of the season, McAvennie and West Ham were big news during 1985/86. A brace on his home debut against Queens Park Rangers, followed by another double soon after against Liverpool, got the ball rolling and in his first 23 games the new boy's enthusiasm was rewarded with 19 goals.

His terrific form continued into the new year, making him a household name. His strikes were the difference in several games as the club achieved an unprecedented third place finish in Division One and went close to winning the league. McAvennie was the Irons' top scorer for the campaign with 26 league goals, a remarkable achievement given the fact he had previously been seen more as a midfielder.

McAVENNIE

Thrust up-front due to injury to Paul Goddard though, he constantly harried defenders and his perfectly-timed runs into the box were finished off in style.

McAvennie's displays, early into his time at the Boleyn Ground, were rewarded in November 1985 with his international debut against Australia at Hampden Park. He scored the second in the 2-0 World Cup qualifying play-off win that put Scotland on their way to the 1986 FIFA World Cup Finals in Mexico.

FULL NAME:
Francis McAvennie

POSITION:
Forward

DATE OF BIRTH:
22 November 1960

PLACE OF BIRTH:
Glasgow

WEST HAM UNITED DEBUT:
First: 17 August 1985
Second: 25 March 1989

APPEARANCES:
190

GOALS:
60

Early the following season, he was soon hitting the target again, striking twice at Old Trafford, when a 3-2 win over the Red Devils put the Hammers top of the embryonic 1986/87 table.

Hopes were high that McAvennie was about to spearhead another tilt at the league championship, but form tailed off and in early October 1987, Celtic came calling.

Back in his home town, McAvennie looked the part once again and with their new record signing in the side, the Bhoys took the Scottish Premier Division by ten points. McAvennie's brace against Dundee United in the Scottish Cup Final completed the double.

Although a Hoops fan growing up, his heart now lay in London. McAvennie placed a transfer request, and before the conclusion of the 1988/89 campaign he was back at the Boleyn, although his return was not enough to prevent relegation. West Ham's record-buy's misfortune continued on the opening day of 1989/90 when he suffered a broken leg during the 1-1 draw at Stoke City.

When he returned to fitness in the spring, the Hammers lay in mid table, eventually finishing seventh and just missing out on the play-offs. Unable to properly oust those ahead of him, he still weighed in with some important goals as the Irons regained their top-flight status a year later. He scored in both Millwall derbies, including a brace in the 3-0 home win, and also grabbed the winner against Barnsley as the run-in picked up pace.

McAVENNIE

However, 1991/92 was disappointing. The momentum from the promotion campaign dissipated, resulting in a swift return to the second tier. The final day did offer some consolation however. McAvennie brought the curtain down on the season, and his Hammers career, bagging a hat-trick in the 3-0 Boleyn Ground triumph over Nottingham Forest.

After a short spell at Aston Villa, several moves later, McAvennie's career came full circle, playing out his final games back at St Mirren.

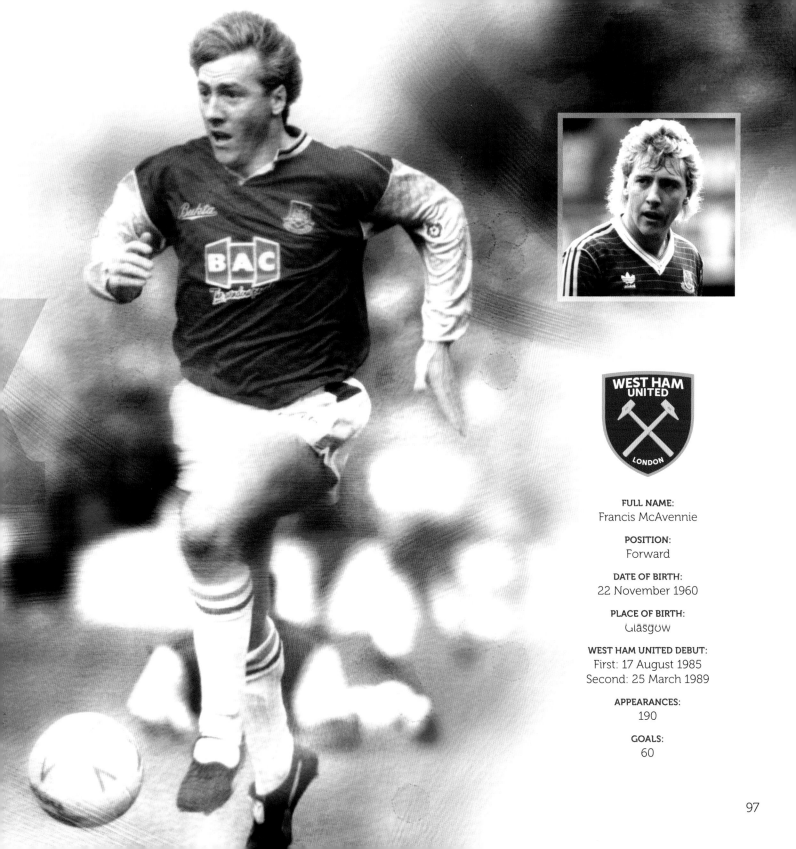

FULL NAME:
Francis McAvennie

POSITION:
Forward

DATE OF BIRTH:
22 November 1960

PLACE OF BIRTH:
Glasgow

WEST HAM UNITED DEBUT:
First: 17 August 1985
Second: 25 March 1989

APPEARANCES:
190

GOALS:
60

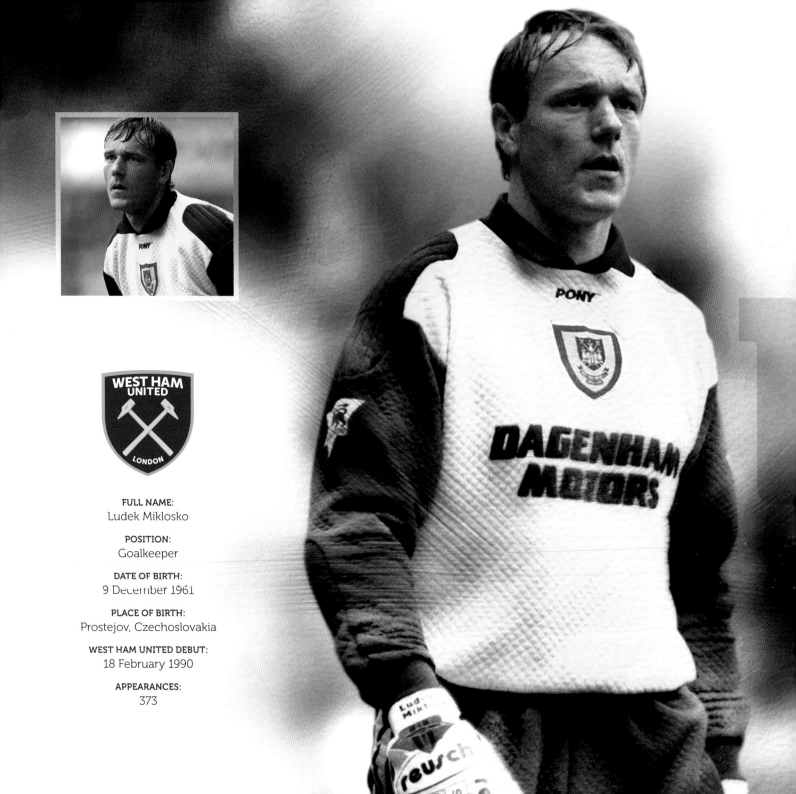

FULL NAME:
Ludek Miklosko

POSITION:
Goalkeeper

DATE OF BIRTH:
9 December 1961

PLACE OF BIRTH:
Prostejov, Czechoslovakia

WEST HAM UNITED DEBUT:
18 February 1990

APPEARANCES:
373

West Ham United fans were delighted to see Ludek Miklosko return to the club he had performed so consistently for as a player, when in 2001, he joined Glenn Roeder's backroom staff as goalkeeping coach.

He spent the next nine years in that position, overseeing several shot-stoppers that were hoping to eclipse Miklosko's own impressive spell as the Hammers' number one for most of the 1990s.

Miklosko first arrived at the club in late 1989, but work permit issues meant he was not authorised to play until the new year. By that point, the man that had brought Miklosko to the club, Lou Macari, was heading for the exit and club legend Billy Bonds was taking over the hot-seat. Miklosko was only on the losing side four times in his first 19 appearances, as the Hammers ended the campaign strongly in seventh, just missing out on a play-off place and enjoying a run to the League Cup semi-finals.

In the summer of 1990, he was off to Italy for the FIFA World Cup as back-up goalkeeper for eventual quarter-finalists, Czechoslovakia. After spending ten years playing senior football in his home country, first with RH Cheb and then at Banik Ostrava, Miklosko made his first international appearance in 1982. He went on to earn 40 caps for Czechoslovakia and a further two for the Czech Republic.

Moving to England for a new challenge and approaching his thirties, he was the prime age for a goalkeeper and once back on domestic duty,

MIKLOSKO

he set about helping the Hammers earn promotion back to Division One. He was also named Hammer of the Year in his first full season at the Boleyn Ground and made the PFA Division Two Team of the Year.

Although just missing out on an FA Cup Final appearance in 1991, when he was part of the side that reached the semi-final, Miklosko did play at Wembley shortly after moving to London, when he featured in the 4-2 international friendly defeat against England.

In 1992/93, Miklosko was again selected for, what was now called, the PFA First Division Team of the Year, as the club returned to the top flight, again finishing as runners-up.

Miklosko was a league ever-present in both promotion efforts, keeping an impressive 21 clean sheets during the first success as the team finished with comfortably, the best defensive record in the division.

Reliable in terms of both performance and availability, he was the club's highest appearance maker in 1990/91, 1993/94 and 1995/96, and was joint highest in both 1994/95 and 1996/97. His statistics also include a fantastic run of 162 consecutive games between March 1992 and December 1995.

The streak both started and effectively ended on Merseyside. The first match came at Anfield against Liverpool and although he was able to play the two games immediately after being sent off, a red card against Everton did eventually lead to suspension.

On 6 May 1997, Miklosko kept his final league clean sheet for the Hammers in a goalless home draw with Newcastle United. He had another shut-out early the following season as the team progressed in the League Cup, beating Huddersfield Town 3-1 over two legs, but a loan move to Queens Park Rangers left him on, an Irons' record, 47 Premier League clean sheets.

MIKLOSKO

Still enjoying life in the capital after almost a decade, the deal at Loftus Road turned into a permanent arrangement and Miklosko's talent again established himself as first choice. QPR were relegated at the end of 2000/01 campaign, but injury had already forced Miklosko to hang up the gloves earlier in the season, paving the way for his second career at the Boleyn Ground.

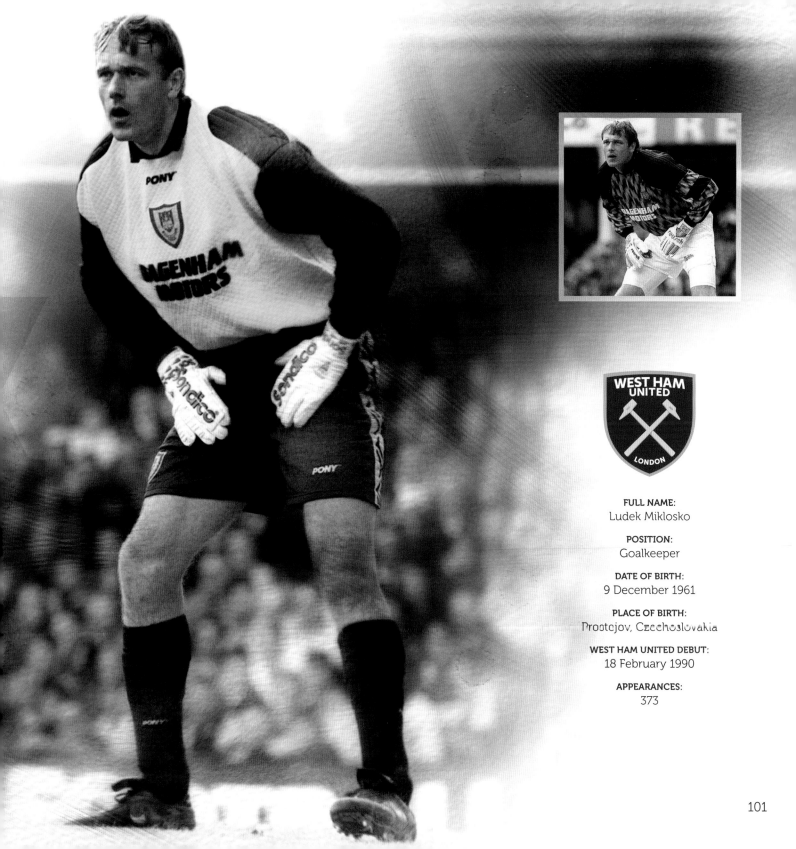

FULL NAME:
Ludek Miklosko

POSITION:
Goalkeeper

DATE OF BIRTH:
9 December 1961

PLACE OF BIRTH:
Prostejov, Czechoslovakia

WEST HAM UNITED DEBUT:
18 February 1990

APPEARANCES:
373

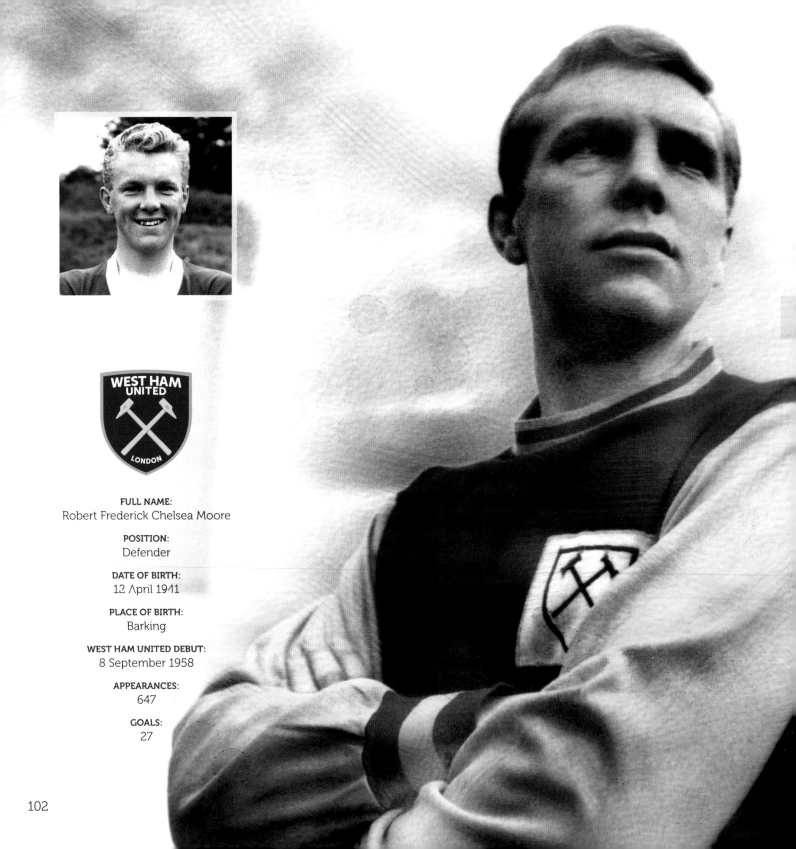

WEST HAM UNITED
LONDON

FULL NAME:
Robert Frederick Chelsea Moore

POSITION:
Defender

DATE OF BIRTH:
12 April 1941

PLACE OF BIRTH:
Barking

WEST HAM UNITED DEBUT:
8 September 1958

APPEARANCES:
647

GOALS:
27

When West Ham United fulfilled their first fixture after Bobby Moore's death in February 1993, a league fixture at Sunderland, an impeccable minute's silence was observed before kick-off at Roker Park.

The tribute paid by both sets of fans that day, was testament to the love and respect all football fans had for Moore. He was not just a Hammers favourite, he was an England hero and a giant of the game.

Over the course of his twenty-year-long playing career, Moore was held in high regard by his peers the world over as one of the very best footballers ever. The immaculate Moore was coolness personified and always seemed to be two steps ahead of everyone else on the pitch. To accompany his ability to read the game and snuff out danger before it really developed, Moore also had the vision and skills to then become the playmaker, quickly turning defence into attack.

Debuting in a home win over Manchester United in 1958, Moore was a first-team regular by the start of the 1960s, despite still being a teenager. Nobody played more times in the famous claret and blue shirt during 1961/62 and 1962/63, and while he did miss a few games towards the end of the next season, he was able to take his rightful place as the Hammers' captain for the 1964 FA Cup Final. The 3-2 victory over Preston North End meant Moore became the first Irons skipper to lift the trophy.

MOORE

Now an established England international, he was also named, the Football Writers' Association Footballer of the Year too.

The FA Cup triumph was the first leg of a wonderful Wembley treble. Twelve months on, he captained the Irons to cup glory again under the twin towers. This time defeating TSV Munich 1860 2-0 to secure the UEFA Cup Winners' Cup, his cross providing Alan Sealey with his second goal of the night.

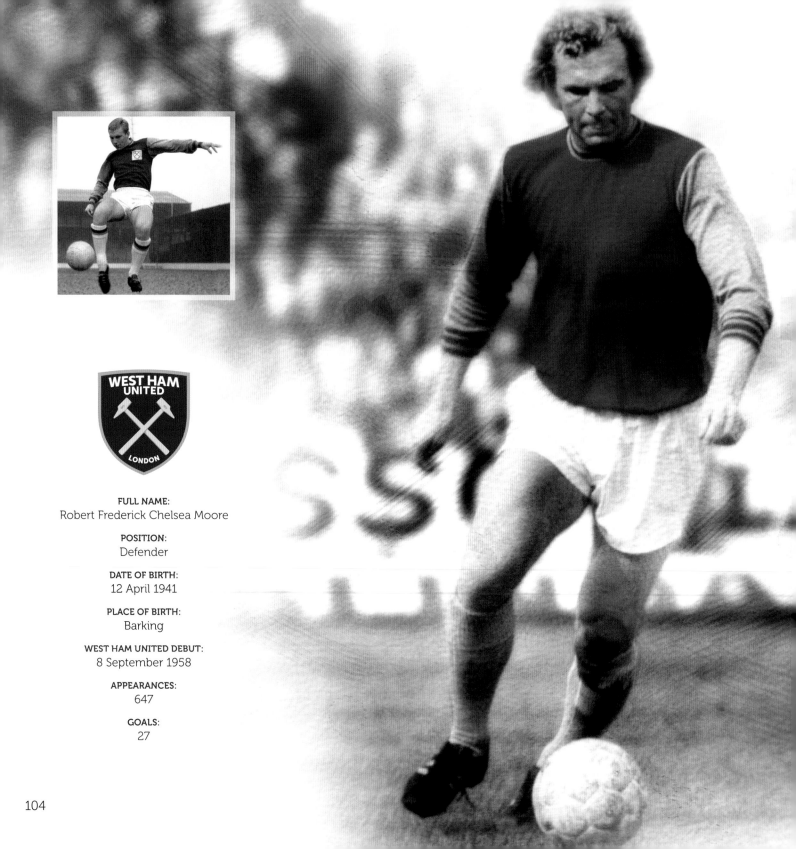

FULL NAME:
Robert Frederick Chelsea Moore

POSITION:
Defender

DATE OF BIRTH:
12 April 1941

PLACE OF BIRTH:
Barking

WEST HAM UNITED DEBUT:
8 September 1958

APPEARANCES:
647

GOALS:
27

In 1966, Moore once again took the now familiar 39 steps up to Wembley's Royal Box, following his superlative performance in England's glorious 4-2 World Cup Final victory over West Germany.

Moore was again the provider, playing the ball through for fellow Hammer, Geoff Hurst's clincher, and creating some of the most enduring images in English football history. Holding aloft the Jules Rimet Trophy led to a string of individual awards as well as being an enormous source of pride to the club.

The first footballer to become BBC Sports Personality of the Year, Moore was awarded an OBE in 1967 and continued to represent his country for another seven years. At the time of his international retirement in 1973, his total of 108 caps was was a national record. Awesome again during the 1970 FIFA World Cup, he was runner-up in the Ballon d'Or and still performing to his own high standards on a domestic level too. He was Hammer of the Year for the fourth time and over the next three seasons, only missed six competitive matches.

Jock Stein's Scottish champions Celtic travelled south in 1970 for Moore's testimonial, an entertaining 3-3 draw, but there was to be no fanfare when Moore played his final game for the Hammers. Injured in a 1974 FA Cup tie against Hereford United, he soon moved to Fulham.

There was an emotional reunion the following season, when the two sides met in the 1975 FA Cup Final at Wembley, Moore this time on the wrong side of the 2-0 scoreline. Despite later enjoying playing spells in America and Denmark, followed by several short stints in management,

MOORE

the names Bobby Moore and West Ham United will always be indelibly linked.

In 1981, playing alongside Pele, Michael Caine and Sylvester Stallone, Moore lined up against the Germans again, escaping to victory as a star of the big screen. Shortly after his death in 1993, a new South Stand at the Boleyn Ground was opened and named in his honour and in 2002, he was an inaugural inductee into the Football Hall of Fame.

His influence and his memory continues to live on through the Bobby Moore Fund for Cancer Research UK.

FULL NAME:
Malcolm Clarke Musgrove

POSITION:
Left-winger

DATE OF BIRTH:
8 July 1933

PLACE OF BIRTH:
Lynemouth

WEST HAM UNITED DEBUT:
27 February 1954

APPEARANCES:
317

GOALS:
98

North East-born Malcolm Musgrove may not have hailed from the capital originally, but some of his most important contributions in a West Ham United shirt were saved for derby games against their London rivals.

His senior debut came against Brentford, he found the back of the Fulham net four times, scored against Orient on four occasions, twice netted against Chelsea, Arsenal and Tottenham Hotspur and once against rivals Millwall. There were also five goals against Charlton Athletic, including a hat-trick in a Southern Floodlight Cup tie in October 1958, but things did not immediately go to plan when Musgrove first secured his place in the team.

Signing for Ted Fenton following his national service with the Royal Air Force, Musgrove did not enjoy victory until his ninth appearance. However, with their new man's wing-play putting the opposition on the back foot, the Irons then won eight of the next eleven games he started, with him scoring in five consecutive matches during that run.

The Hammers earned their top-flight place on the final day of the 1957/58 season, Musgrove grabbing the third in the 3-1 victory over Middlesbrough in the North East. In addition to his Division Two title winners' medal that season, he also played in the Essex Professional Cup Final 4-1 triumph over Leyton Orient in 1959.

Musgrove's keen eye for goal gave him a better strike rate than some orthodox forwards of the time. He was named Hammer of the Year

MUSGROVE

for the 1959/60 season when he was the club's top scorer and almost two years to the day after his first hat-trick against the Addicks, he cracked in another treble in the 5-2 Division One thrashing of Preston North End.

He later moved to Brisbane Road as a player-coach in 1962, the same year he became chairman of the Professional Footballers' Association, and worked with several other clubs before his retirement in 1998.

FULL NAME:
Mark James Noble

POSITION:
Midfielder

DATE OF BIRTH:
8 May 1987

PLACE OF BIRTH:
Canning Town

WEST HAM UNITED DEBUT:
24 August 2004

APPEARANCES:
376*

GOALS:
44*

*CORRECT AS OF 25 SEPTEMBER 2016

One of the club's favourite sons, Club Captain and the squad's longest serving player, Mark Noble is West Ham United through and through.

An England captain at youth levels and another graduate of the Academy, Noble was technically proficient from a young age and it still shows now, with his consistently impressive performances.

In February 2003, an appearance for West Ham's reserve side while only 15 years of age, gave a very early indication as to the temperament of Noble. At the time, he had not even started his full-time apprenticeship with the club, yet eleven years later he became the Hammers' highest appearance maker in the Premier League. A statistic even more impressive, given that West Ham have not always been in the top flight during Noble's time. After two substitute appearances in the League Cup during 2004/05, his first league games came in the Championship.

Promotion was sealed in the Play-Off Final at the Millennium Stadium though and Noble, a late substitute in the win over Preston North End, was named Young Hammer of the Year in his first season of senior football.

The following campaign, Noble had spells back in the Championship, on loan to Hull City and Ipswich Town, but soon after Alan Curbishley's arrival as manager halfway through 2006/07, he firmly established himself in the first eleven.

NOBLE

Curbishley, himself a former Hammers midfielder, and his hot-seat successors, have all come to rely upon Noble running things from the middle of the park. An accurate passer with a great engine, as well as a dependable penalty taker.

Noble's first spot-kick secured all three points against Birmingham City in August 2007 and when he netted twice from twelve yards in the 3-1 defeat of Watford in April 2016, it became the fourth occasion he had achieved the feat.

Injured for the 2010/11 run-in when the Irons were relegated, Noble was instrumental in bringing the club straight back up. The Hammer of the Year, who was also included in the PFA Championship Team of the Year, missed only three matches all season and appeared in another Play-Off Final win, this time beating Blackpool 2-1 in dramatic fashion.

His battling role against Blackpool was vital, showing the grit and determination Irons' fans expect from one of their own. More than comfortable in the first two seasons back in the big time, Noble ended 2013/14 as Hammer of the Year for a second time. The following campaign, Noble eclipsed Steve Potts' total of 204 Premier League games and it was appropriate that one of the Hammers' most dedicated players was given the honour of skippering the West Ham United's final campaign at the Boleyn Ground.

With Noble overseeing proceedings, the final season was a great one. The side started the season brilliantly with wins at big-guns Arsenal, Liverpool and Manchester City, finishing in seventh place in the Premier League and qualifying for Europe.

In March 2016, Noble's loyalty was rewarded with the last ever testimonial game to be held at the Boleyn Ground. Noble's West Ham XI took on a Hammers all-stars side, which included the likes of David James, Teddy Sheringham, Paolo Di Canio, Michael Carrick and Rio Ferdinand.

NOBLE

In the thrilling encounter, Noble got himself on the score-sheet early on, before former teammate Dean Ashton netted an absolute beauty, a stunning overhead kick from an Ian Bishop cross.

Twelve years on and still a great servant to the club, there is still plenty more to come from Mark Noble.

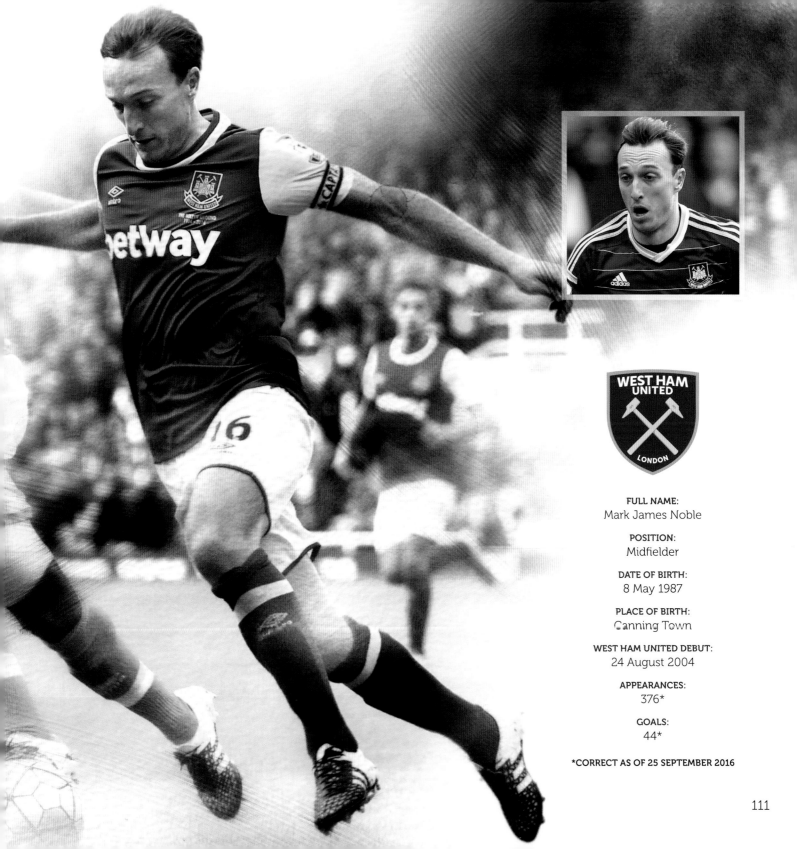

FULL NAME:
Mark James Noble

POSITION:
Midfielder

DATE OF BIRTH:
8 May 1987

PLACE OF BIRTH:
Canning Town

WEST HAM UNITED DEBUT:
24 August 2004

APPEARANCES:
376*

GOALS:
44*

*CORRECT AS OF 25 SEPTEMBER 2016

FULL NAME:
Graham Charles Paddon

POSITION:
Midfielder

DATE OF BIRTH:
24 August 1950

PLACE OF BIRTH:
Manchester

WEST HAM UNITED DEBUT:
8 December 1973

APPEARANCES:
152

GOALS:
15

During the mid-1970s, Graham Paddon was a vital cog in Ron Greenwood's midfield machine and despite playing alongside legends such as Billy Bonds and Trevor Brooking, he was never overshadowed by the distinguished company he kept.

Signing in a big money plus player deal, which took Ted MacDougall to Carrow Road, Paddon had been a success at Norwich City and later returned to the Canaries, after an even more successful stay at Upton Park.

A Division Two champion with City in 1972, Paddon played in the League Cup Final the following season. Lining up alongside another future Hammer David Cross, he tasted defeat at the hands of Tottenham Hotspur that day, but the experience put him in good stead for another Wembley appearance two seasons later.

As so often happens, Paddon's first goals for his new club were against his old one. The Irons defeated Norwich 4-2 on New Year's Day 1974 and slowly began pulling away from relegation trouble, transforming the following season into FA Cup winners.

A fine influence in the middle of the park, Paddon's strikes were often corkers. A volley against Arsenal five days before the cup final, ensured the Hammers lined up against Fulham in high spirits, and after winning underneath the twin towers, he fired in another screamer against Eintracht Frankfurt in the resulting UEFA Cup Winners' Cup campaign.

Paddon also gained international honours in 1975/76, featuring as an over-age player for England's U23s, alongside clubmate Kevin Lock. Despite scoring in the 3-1 win against Hungary, the result was not

PADDON

enough for the national side to progress in the European Championships and the match proved to be England's last at U23 level.

The following season, Paddon headed back to Norfolk, only to suffer a broken leg in only his third game back in yellow and green, which kept him out for almost a year.

Following the 1977/78 campaign, he enjoyed a summer loan spell stateside with Tampa Bay Rowdies and a short stint back home with Millwall, before moving to Hong Kong to represent Eastern AA.

London boy Scott Parker has spent the majority of his career playing for clubs in the capital and excelled during his four seasons at the Boleyn Ground.

Breaking onto the scene at Charlton Athletic, the tenacious central midfielder had a short loan at Norwich City before making a big-money switch to Chelsea in January 2004. His powerful displays earned him the 2003/04 PFA Young Player of the Year accolade, but following some high-profile signings at Stamford Bridge and first team opportunities being limited, Parker took the road north to Newcastle. A stand-out performer for the Magpies, his arrival at West Ham United was seen as a something of a coup, although injury did hamper his initial progress.

After missing the start of the 2007/08 season, Parker was then ruled out for a further two months, after coming off at half-time during his league debut at home to Arsenal. Once fit again and playing the holding role, he was soon making a major impression in the Hammers' midfield, influencing the flow of games and swinging momentum in the Irons' favour.

Ultra dependable, Parker was named Hammer of the Year three seasons on the spin. The latter two campaigns were a struggle for the side though and while Parker helped drag the club to safety in 2009/10, with a vital goal against Wigan Athletic, survival went down to the wire and relegation eventually caught up with the Hammers in 2010/11.

Despite the drop, Parker's performances went from strength to strength and he received a string of individual awards. The first Hammer since Bobby Moore to be the Football Writers' Footballer of the Year,

PARKER

his stock was high and a recall to the England squad was his reward.

As well as going down, the club had been knocked out in the latter stages of both cup competitions and their disappointment continued when Parker left for Tottenham Hotspur at the start of the following season. West Ham made a swift return to the top flight and after two seasons at White Hart Lane, Parker moved across London to Fulham.

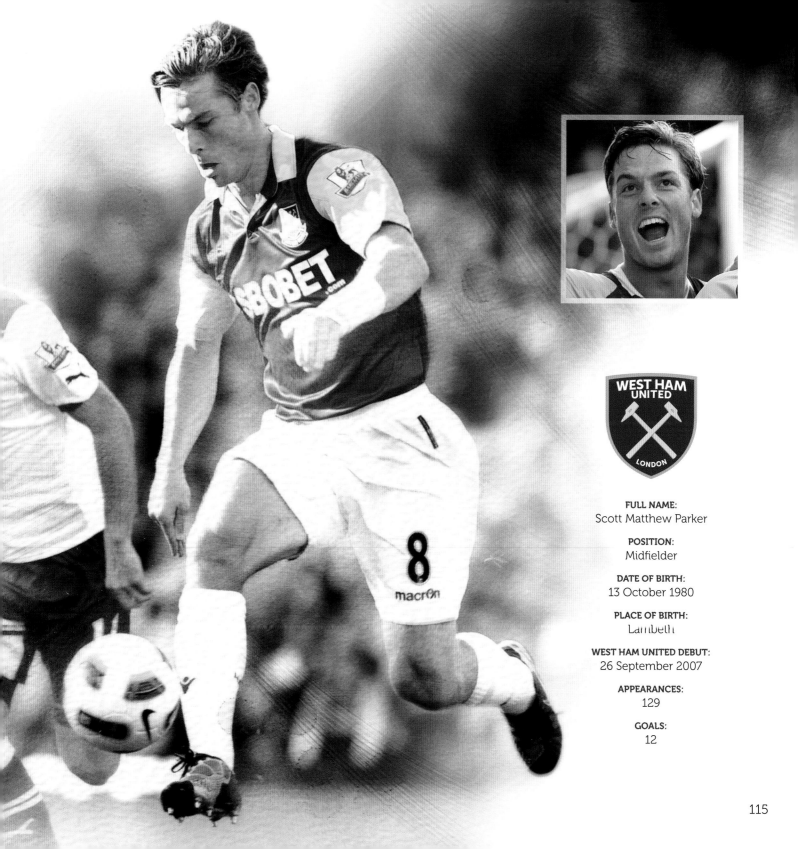

FULL NAME:
Scott Matthew Parker

POSITION:
Midfielder

DATE OF BIRTH:
13 October 1980

PLACE OF BIRTH:
Lambeth

WEST HAM UNITED DEBUT:
26 September 2007

APPEARANCES:
129

GOALS:
12

After starting out at Walsall, Phil Parkes moved to Queens Park Rangers and established himself as one of the country's best stoppers, making 344 league appearances for the Hoops.

Such an accomplishment would normally be considered as someone having had a very successful career, but for Phil Parkes, this was only half the story. He then went on to play exactly the same amount of league games for West Ham United, a true testament to his outstanding ability between the sticks.

Parkes' longevity owed much to his sharp reflexes and assured handling. An imposing figure, he was an integral part of the QPR side that pushed Liverpool all the way, in the race for the Division One title in 1976.

Two years earlier, he had made his England debut in an experimental line-up against Portugal. The friendly international staged in Lisbon ended goalless and Parkes' clean sheets were to become his stock-in-trade for the Hammers.

In 1979, Irons' manager John Lyall spent a world record fee for a goalkeeper to get his new number one. Parkes dropped down a division to become a Hammer, but was soon joined by his former employers when the Hoops were relegated at the end of the season.

Both in Division Two for 1979/80, it was the Loftus Road club that finished the higher of the two sides, but Parkes had bigger things on

PARKES

his mind. His new side were looking forward to a Wembley FA Cup Final against Arsenal and thanks to his shut-out and a Trevor Brooking header, there were claret and blue ribbons on the famous trophy that day.

The following season proved to be a marathon and Parkes was involved every step of the way, maintaining his ever-present tag throughout and playing in a mammoth 61 games.

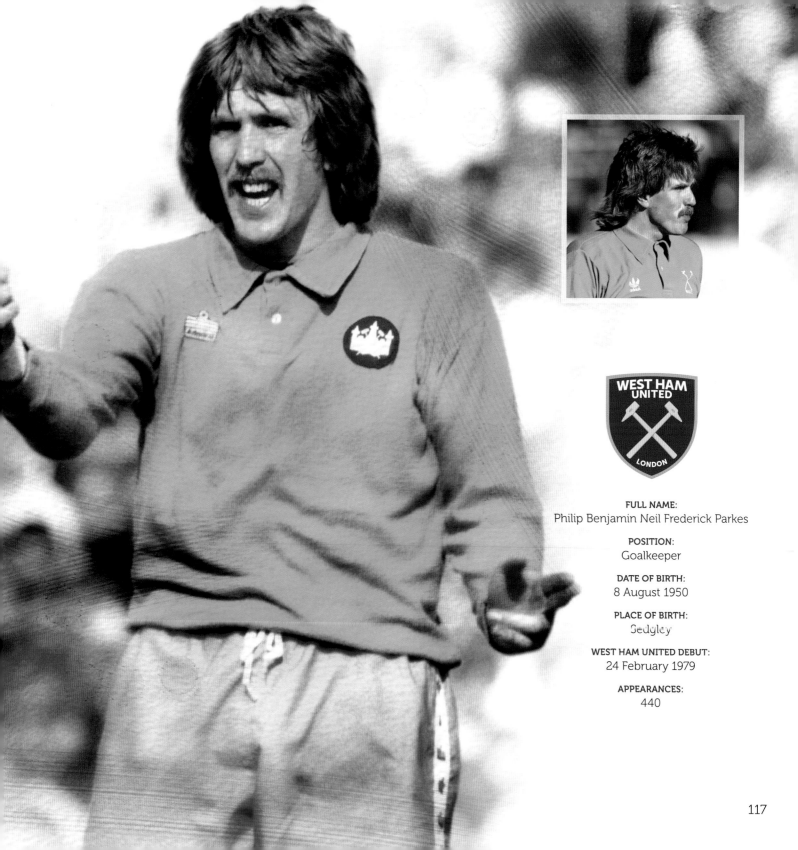

FULL NAME:
Philip Benjamin Neil Frederick Parkes

POSITION:
Goalkeeper

DATE OF BIRTH:
8 August 1950

PLACE OF BIRTH:
Sedgley

WEST HAM UNITED DEBUT:
24 February 1979

APPEARANCES:
440

117

League Cup finalists and UEFA Cup Winners' Cup quarter-finalists with Parkes as the final line of defence, West Ham swept aside all before them in Division Two, including, of course, QPR.

The Hammers headed to the top of the table following the 5-0 rout of Bristol City in November 1980 and stayed there for the remainder of the campaign. The Hammers' defensive record was one of the cornerstones of the success and the clean sheet against the Robins was one of 22 in the league and 29 in total, giving Parkes the club record for the most clean sheets in a season.

His performances were rewarded with him being named in the PFA Division Two Team of the Year for the second season running, and in a campaign where there was no shortage of candidates, Parkes was declared Hammer of the Year.

Back in the top flight in 1981/82, Parkes kept the opposition at bay on a further ten occasions as the side achieved a credible top-half finish. In all, he had 146 clean sheets, of which 114 came in the league, seeing him top the club's list in both categories.

Ever-present again in 1982/83 and 1983/84, injury resulted in him missing the majority of the following season, before once more playing every game the season after that - third place in 1985/86 proving to be the Hammers' best ever league finish.

After initially being phased out of the team, Parkes' recall towards the end of 1988/89 came too late to stave off relegation and although he

PARKES

retained his place at the start of the following campaign, it proved to be his last at the Boleyn Ground.

Reuniting with John Lyall, Parkes played three games for Ipswich Town before joining the coaching staff. It was the Tractor Boys that provided the opposition for Parkes' testimonial just before the beginning of 1990/91. The game finished 1-1, but with Parkes playing a half for each side, it came as no surprise that he was unbeaten in both.

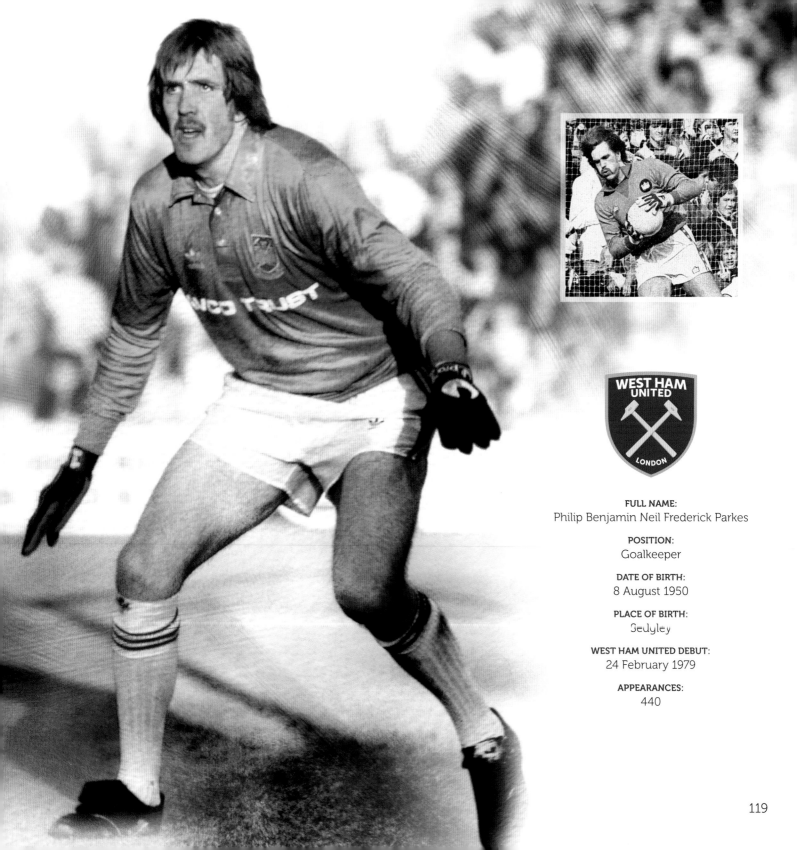

FULL NAME:
Philip Benjamin Neil Frederick Parkes

POSITION:
Goalkeeper

DATE OF BIRTH:
8 August 1950

PLACE OF BIRTH:
Sedgley

WEST HAM UNITED DEBUT:
24 February 1979

APPEARANCES:
440

119

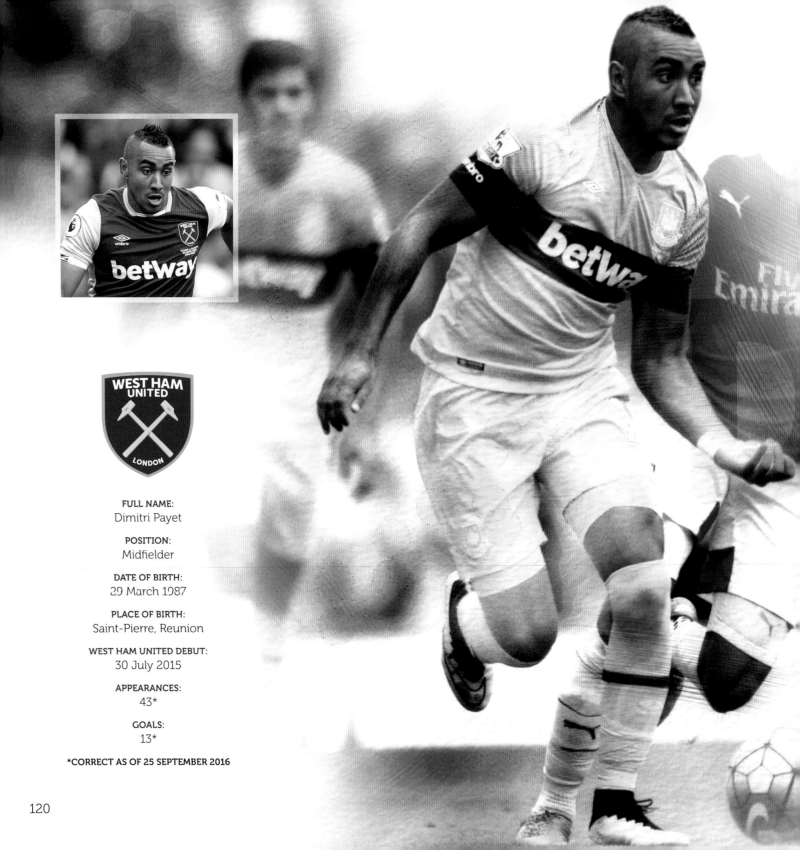

FULL NAME:
Dimitri Payet

POSITION:
Midfielder

DATE OF BIRTH:
29 March 1987

PLACE OF BIRTH:
Saint-Pierre, Reunion

WEST HAM UNITED DEBUT:
30 July 2015

APPEARANCES:
43*

GOALS:
13*

*CORRECT AS OF 25 SEPTEMBER 2016

Arriving at the Boleyn Ground before the start of the 2015/16 campaign from Olympic Marseille, Dimitri Payet became West Ham United's newest hero after a stunning debut season in the Premier League.

Payet produced a wealth of eye-catching displays for the Hammers, earning himself a place in the PFA Team of the Year, after taking to the speed and intensity of English football brilliantly.

With the ability to put goalscoring opportunities on a plate for his teammates, Payet's vision and mesmeric ball skills had supporters on their feet and the opposition defenders in knots. Converting chances that came his way was no problem either, indeed he also scored enough beauties to have his own Goal of the Season competition.

A free-kick specialist, his precisely placed shot against Newcastle United and a deft chip against Crystal Palace helped West Ham's season get off to a flyer. After missing the Christmas period through injury, Payet came back in the New Year to devastating effect.

He was breathtaking away at Bournemouth and against Blackburn Rovers in the FA Cup, Payet delighted the vast number of travelling Irons with another trademark free-kick, before capping off his virtuoso display with a late solo run and finish.

With the game seemingly lost at Everton, Payet turned it round, snatching a dramatic winner in a 3-2 victory, having earlier created the equaliser. He then scored twice more in his next three Hammers games, including another superb effort against Palace.

PAYET

As well as endearing himself to the Boleyn faithful, Payet's form saw him recalled to the France squad, allowing him to showcase his outstanding talents at UEFA Euro 2016.

Man of the Match in two group games and one of the stars of the tournament, as the hosts reached the final, he continued his superb form into the following season with another peach of a free-kick to give West Ham victory over Accrington Stanley in their first domestic cup-tie at London Stadium.

Martin Peters was the type of player that made playing football look easy, but the glittering career of this West Ham United youth product is down to plenty of hard work and commitment too.

Peters made his senior bow during the busy Easter period of 1962 and having never played for the first team before, suddenly enjoyed five games in ten days. A comprehensive 4-1 victory on his debut against Cardiff City on Good Friday was quickly followed by an entertaining 3-3 draw with Arsenal 24 hours later. Peters went on to score five goals against the Gunners in West Ham colours, but in the return match against Cardiff, it was the goalkeeper's jersey he had to pull on.

Featuring in only his third match, Peters bravely put his hand up to fill in when Brian Rhodes was injured at Ninian Park and while the Irons went on to lose, he put up a good showing. With his versatility and willingness, he was an invaluable player to have in the side during the era of first, no substitutions and then only one, but it also made him vulnerable to being dropped when specialised players returned.

It meant that during 1963/64, despite having experienced well over 50 games for the club, Peters did not feature at all in the winning FA Cup run. Selected for the final league game of the season, when other players were rested before the Preston North End showpiece, he made sure he was not going to miss out on glory the following season.

PETERS

After three consecutive defeats which had seen the team slump down the early 1964/65 Division One table, Peters returned to the first team and played his part in the 5-0 Boleyn Ground thrashing of Wolverhampton Wanderers.

Elegant with the ball and constantly on the move, Peters did not put a foot wrong as he ran the show during the 1965 UEFA Cup Winners' Cup Final victory against TSV Munich 1860.

WEST HAM UNITED LONDON

FULL NAME:
Martin Stanford Peters MBE

POSITION:
Midfielder

DATE OF BIRTH:
8 November 1943

PLACE OF BIRTH:
Plaistow

WEST HAM UNITED DEBUT:
20 April 1962

APPEARANCES:
364

GOALS:
100

The following season, having played more times for the Hammers than anyone else and grabbing the attention of England manager Alf Ramsey, Peters returned to Wembley for the 1966 FIFA World Cup Final beating of West Germany.

Peters, like clubmate Geoff Hurst, who converted Peters' inch-perfect cross for the only goal of the quarter-final against Argentina, had only just arrived onto the international scene during the build up to the tournament, but his style suited England's new tactics perfectly.

Peters' goal in the famous final of 1966 edged England ahead and looked like being the winner, before a late Wolfgang Weber goal forced extra-time. Hurst completed his hat-trick, England were World Champions and the rest is history. The image of captain Bobby Moore holding the Jules Rimet trophy aloft on the shoulders of Geoff Hurst and Ray Wilson, with Martin Peters alongside, remains immortalised only yards from the Boleyn Ground.

Peters had also been on target in a final prior to the World Cup success, having netted during the second leg of the League Cup Final against West Bromwich Albion, and while it was not enough to stop the Baggies winning 5-3 on aggregate, he did have the consolation of scoring his only Hammers hat-trick against them in a 4-0 victory at the Boleyn Ground in August 1968.

Having twice scored against the Throstles before the League Cup Final, the treble went towards a further seven against them while still playing for the Hammers, and either side of the 1967/68 and 1968/69 campaigns

PETERS

he totalled 14 goals in 17 games. Peters then racked up his century of West Ham strikes with a brace in a 3-2 win against Sheffield Wednesday at Hillsborough in early 1970, which proved to be his last goals for the club.

Moving to Tottenham Hotspur he enjoyed further success, winning domestic and European medals, before signing for former teammate John Bond at Norwich City. He received an MBE in 1978 and still remains a regular at Hammers games.

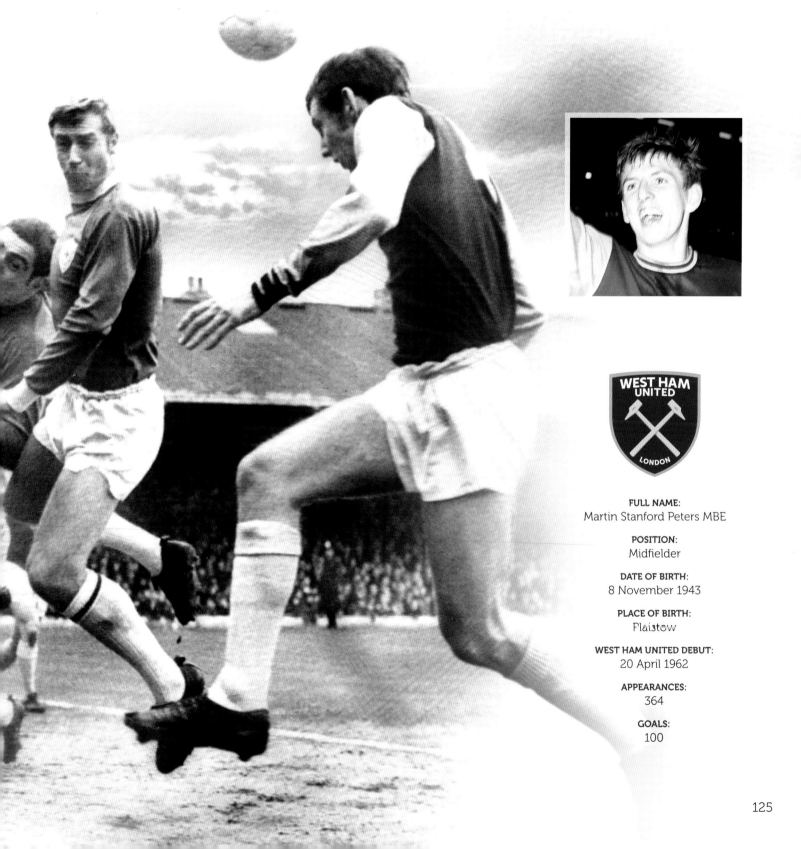

FULL NAME:
Martin Stanford Peters MBE

POSITION:
Midfielder

DATE OF BIRTH:
8 November 1943

PLACE OF BIRTH:
Plaistow

WEST HAM UNITED DEBUT:
20 April 1962

APPEARANCES:
364

GOALS:
100

FULL NAME:
Geoff Pike

POSITION:
Midfielder

DATE OF BIRTH:
28 September 1956

PLACE OF BIRTH:
Clapton

WEST HAM UNITED DEBUT:
6 March 1976

APPEARANCES:
368

GOALS:
41

After being spotted by West Ham United playing local boys football, Geoff Pike appeared for the club in the 1975 FA Youth Cup Final, five years before walking out at Wembley in the senior version of the same competition.

Graduating through the youth ranks and making a handful of promising first team appearances, Pike's footballing education continued with two campaigns in the North American Soccer League in 1976 and 1977. Turning out for the Hartford Bicentennials, who then moved to New Haven and renamed Connecticut, Pike was playing for a side with one of the smallest budgets in the Atlantic Conference, but returned all the better for it.

Utilised in several different positions, his great stamina meant Pike matured into a midfield regular during the 1979/80 season and featured in the Hammers' 1-0 FA Cup Final win over Arsenal, having started the run by scoring the winner in the 2-1 third round replay win over West Bromwich Albion at the Boleyn Ground. The following season, Pike was ever-present as the team reached the League Cup Final, UEFA Cup Winners' Cup quarter-final and won the Division Two title with ease, scoring in three consecutive games in April 1981 as West Ham kicked on during the run-in.

Pike weighed in with more goals as West Ham resumed their top-flight status, scoring against Merseyside giants Liverpool two seasons running. He started 1983 with a New Year's Day goal in the 3-0 home win over Spurs and then ended the year with another, as the Irons defeated their arch-rivals Arsenal 3-1.

PIKE

The Gunners were beaten at home by the same scoreline the next season and once again, Pike was on target, but in his final two campaigns, his appearances were restricted and he signed off with a deserved testimonial against Dynamo Zagreb at the end of 1987/88. He moved on to Notts Country before returning to London to play for Leyton Orient and then non-league Hendon.

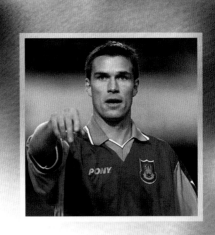

FULL NAME:
Steven John Potts

POSITION:
Defender

DATE OF BIRTH:
7 May 1967

PLACE OF BIRTH:
Hartford, United States of America

WEST HAM UNITED DEBUT:
1 January 1985

APPEARANCES:
506

GOALS:
1

A cult hero and defensive rock with 16 years in the first team squad, Steve Potts became one of West Ham United's longest serving players and one of their highest appearance makers too.

Having won the league with the Hammers youth team, he made his senior debut aged 18, when manager John Lyall was forced to shuffle the squad due to injuries. Played in midfield, Potts would soon get used to slotting in where needed. At that point he was primarily played as a right-back and now knowing the required level to excel, he captained the successful reserve team while patiently waiting for his chance.

His first prolonged spell in the first team arrived during 1988/89, but again, the adaptable Potts was often asked to switch roles. He was even pushed up front during the 1990/91 Division Two promotion campaign, the season in which he had scored his only Irons goal, before finding his true calling the following term.

One of the few success stories during relegation, he proved to be a natural centre-back and his pace and positional play, meant his lack of height was rarely an issue. Potts was given the captain's armband the following season, as the Irons quickly returned to the top flight.

His commanding displays earned him the Hammer of the Year prize and during the following two campaigns he only missed one game, a win over Oldham Athletic three days after the birth of his son Daniel, before again being named the Hammer of the Year for 1994/95.

POTTS

In 1997, goals from Ian Bishop and Steve Lomas ensured the Boleyn faithful were celebrating Potts' testimonial with a 2-0 victory over Queens Park Rangers and during his final season in 2000/01, he passed the 500 game milestone. Ten years later, he also had the pleasure of watching his son Daniel play for the club he loved, before he moved on to Luton Town in 2015.

After joining West Ham United in February 1971, 'Pop' Robson did not miss a game until October 1973, and during his two spells with the Hammers, he did not miss the target much either.

Starting out with Newcastle United, Robson soon showed his predatory instincts and having helped fire them to the 1964/65 Division Two title, he remains in the Magpies' all-time top ten scoring charts.

A real goal-poacher, he still found the net on a regular basis in the top flight, which led to him becoming the Hammers' record buy in 1971 when he relocated to the capital. Robson made the perfect start to life at the Boleyn Ground, scoring the first on his debut in a routine 2-0 win over Nottingham Forest. In general, the team had been struggling and Robson's arrival was a big step towards them maintaining their Division One status, with important goals against Manchester United and West Bromwich Albion securing maximum points.

Behind only Geoff Hurst and Clyde Best in the Hammers' scoring charts for 1971/72, it was the following season when Robson really cut loose. He was awarded the Golden Boot at the end of the 1972/73 campaign for being Division One's top goalscorer and earned the title, Hammer of the Year.

All Robson's 28 goals that campaign, came in the league. He also set a club record for braces scored in a season with eight doubles, all but one taking place at the Boleyn Ground.

ROBSON

This included two in a 2-2 Boxing Day draw with Tottenham Hotspur plus two in a welcome 3-1 win over another London rival, Chelsea.

In addition to the two-goal hauls, he went one better with a hat-trick in a 4-3 win over Southampton, his last goals of the campaign and the team's last victory in a season where the club ended up with a very healthy sixth-place finish.

FULL NAME:
Bryan Stanley Robson

POSITION:
Forward

DATE OF BIRTH:
11 November 1945

PLACE OF BIRTH:
Sunderland

WEST HAM UNITED DEBUT:
First: 24 February 1971
Second: 16 October 1976

APPEARANCES:
255

GOALS:
104

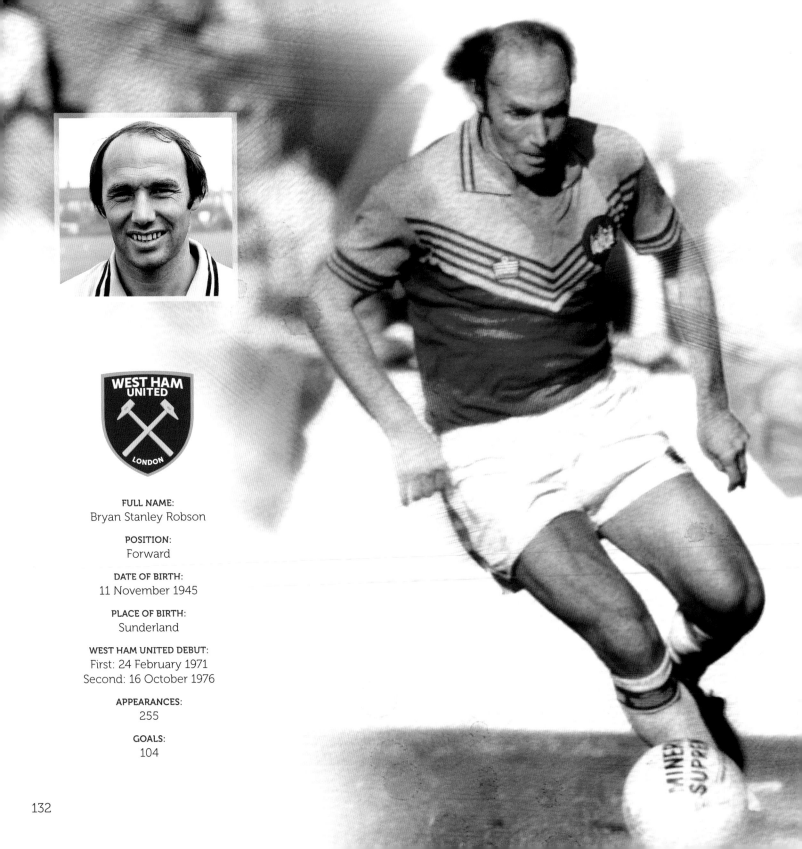

FULL NAME:
Bryan Stanley Robson

POSITION:
Forward

DATE OF BIRTH:
11 November 1945

PLACE OF BIRTH:
Sunderland

WEST HAM UNITED DEBUT:
First: 24 February 1971
Second: 16 October 1976

APPEARANCES:
255

GOALS:
104

At the time of Robson's West Ham United goalscoring exploits, his hometown team were busy pulling off an improbable FA Cup winning campaign, and it was north at Sunderland where he would start the 1974/75 season.

The switch meant he missed the Hammers' own FA Cup success, but the following season, Robson did get another Division Two winners' medal with the Black Cats. He was top scorer for the club during his two full seasons at Roker Park, but in October 1976, made the return journey to London to rejoin the Irons.

Sunderland were relegated after only one season and a year later West Ham joined them back in Division Two, despite the team winning six of the last nine fixtures and Robson, top scorer again, giving the Hammers hope with two goals in a late season win over Derby County.

'Pop', so called due to a childhood nickname, was small, but powerful and had a great touch. Playing once more in the second tier, he made it a pair of Golden Boots after finishing 1978/79 as the division's top scorer. His account included a terrific hat-trick in a 3-0 win over Millwall, having also scored both goals in the previous home win over Sheffield United.

Robson ended his Hammers career just as he started it, with a goal, scoring in his final appearance with another against Millwall, before again returning to Wearside for the 1979/80 season.

ROBSON

It meant he missed more West Ham FA Cup glory, but two days after the Hammers had beaten Arsenal at Wembley, the new cup holders had to fulfil their remaining league fixture at Roker Park. Robson helped Sunderland to another promotion-securing victory ensuring both sides had something to celebrate.

Playing also for Carlisle United, Chelsea and Gateshead, Robson squeezed in another Sunderland homecoming, before becoming a respected coach and scout.

A quick-fire brace in the 1965 UEFA Cup Winners' Cup Final gave West Ham United their first European trophy and ensured that Alan Sealey would always be a part of the Irons' proud history.

Sealey had made the short move from Orient in 1961, during the period in-between the Ted Fenton and Ron Greenwood tenures. He was brought in as part of a swap-deal involving Dave Dunmore, despite having only a handful of senior appearances behind him. The club's directors saw his potential and were rewarded as he quickly forced his way into the first team. After scoring twice on his Football Combination debut, he featured as the central striker in the last six Division One games of the campaign, netting his first goal in a 1-1 draw at home to Manchester City.

During 1962/63, Greenwood experimented, using Sealey behind or wider than the main forward and it suited him. He scored late-season braces against Leicester City and the Citizens, before taking his place in the squad that visited the United States of America and won the International Soccer League.

Despite scoring in the League Cup semi-final first leg against the eventual trophy-winners Leicester City, Sealey was overlooked for the 1964 FA Cup win that same season. He remained on the fringes during 1964/65 too, but on the night of the 2-0 win over TSV Munich 1860, everything fell into place. Having already scored against Sparta in the second round, his three minute, second-half double in the high-class Wembley encounter not only won the cup for the Hammers, but secured a place in Hammers history for Sealey.

SEALEY

After such a high, Sealey then suffered extreme misfortune. Following a promising pre-season for the new hero, which included another goal against 1860 back in America, he broke his leg during an impromptu cricket knockabout and missed over a year of football.

Sealey's eventual return to first team colours came in December 1966 in the 3-0 home win over West Bromwich Albion, but he only made four league appearances during the whole of the 1966/67 campaign, ending his Hammers career on the final day of the season, in a draw against Manchester City at the Boleyn Ground.

FULL NAME:
Alan William Sealey

POSITION:
Forward

DATE OF BIRTH:
22 April 1942

PLACE OF BIRTH:
Hampton

WEST HAM UNITED DEBUT:
3 April 1961

APPEARANCES:
128

GOALS:
26

FULL NAME:
John Sissons

POSITION:
Forward

DATE OF BIRTH:
30 September 1945

PLACE OF BIRTH:
Hayes

WEST HAM UNITED DEBUT:
4 May 1963

APPEARANCES:
266

GOALS:
53

John Sissons was an exciting footballer with outstanding talent and one of several integral members of West Ham United's team during the glory years of the mid-1960s.

Playing just two days short of the first anniversary of his league debut, Sissons' trusty left foot made him the youngest player to have scored in an FA Cup Final, when he got the Hammers' first goal against Preston North End in 1964. A year later, after scoring in the semi-final second leg 1-1 draw in Spain against Real Zaragoza, Sissons was also in the victorious Hammers team that lifted the UEFA Cup Winners' Cup at Wembley.

Pacy, direct and full of tricks, Sissons continued to chip in with goals throughout his career. In November 1966, he notched a hat-trick in a 7-0 League Cup humiliation of Leeds United and grabbed two more against the Pensioners in a crazy 5-5 draw the following month.

In 1967, Sissons took part in West Ham's London Five-A-Side Football Championship win and at the end of the year, his strike at Filbert Street meant the team had beaten Leicester City by the same 4-2 score line twice in four days.

His half-century of goals for the club included two efforts against Sheffield Wednesday, the team he joined in 1970. Four years later he moved to Norwich City to play for former Hammer John Bond, but left shortly after to sign for Chelsea, who were relegated from Division One at the same time the Canaries were going up.

SISSONS

Sissons then moved to the North American Soccer League, winning Soccer Bowl 75 with Tampa Bay Rowdies alongside former Hammers teammate Clyde Best, before ending his playing days with Cape Town City in South Africa, where in 1976, he was part of the National Football League and Castle Cup double-winning team.

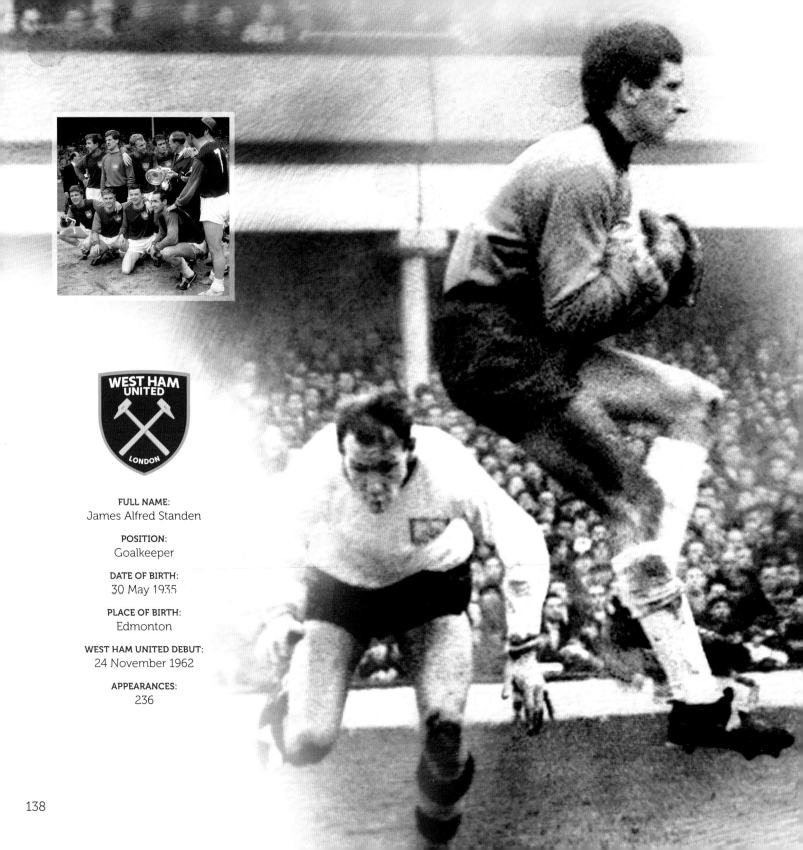

FULL NAME:
James Alfred Standen

POSITION:
Goalkeeper

DATE OF BIRTH:
30 May 1935

PLACE OF BIRTH:
Edmonton

WEST HAM UNITED DEBUT:
24 November 1962

APPEARANCES:
236

Having been used primarily as an understudy at Arsenal and Luton Town, Jim Standen arrived at West Ham United as cover for the injured Lawrie Leslie, yet he played so well for the Hammers that he made the number one jersey his own.

Helping form the spine of the team noted for its attacking qualities, he made sure his last line of defence was kept tight and in the mid-1960s was prominent in both cup campaigns, as the Hammers won their first two major honours.

Shutting out Charlton Athletic and Orient in the early rounds of the 1964 FA Cup, plus keeping clean sheets in the UEFA Cup Winners' Cup against Gent, Sparta Prague and in the final against TSV Munich 1860 the following season, Standen's role was substantial.

Strong and reliable under pressure and good with his angles, the busy Standen was not only a dependable goalkeeper, but an all-year-round sportsman, spending his summers wielding the willow, firstly in minor counties cricket, before making his first-class debut for Worcestershire in 1962.

The following year, he missed their Gillette Cup Final to play in goal for the Irons at Sheffield United instead, but in the same year he picked up his FA Cup winners' medal, the right-arm medium pacer bowled his way to the County Championship title and another winners' medal.

His Hammers career had started against Sheffield Wednesday and his last appearance for the club came against their city rivals United.

STANDEN

Upon his departure from the Boleyn Ground in 1967, Standen moved to the United States for a spell with Detroit Cougars, retuning home for stints with Millwall and Portsmouth before hanging up his gloves in 1972.

FULL NAME:
Raymond Struan McDonald Stewart

POSITION:
Defender

DATE OF BIRTH:
7 September 1959

PLACE OF BIRTH:
Stanley, Scotland

WEST HAM UNITED DEBUT:
4 September 1979

APPEARANCES:
432

GOALS:
84

Although Ray Stewart is famously, the only non-Englishman to represent West Ham United in a FA Cup Final winning side, the Boleyn faithful took him, and his all-action style, to their hearts as if he was one of their own.

A fearless, stubborn right-back, Stewart's talents were highly sought after among several Scottish clubs when he joined Dundee United from local boys football, having already represented his country at youth level. His burgeoning reputation grew at Tannadice Park. Following his senior debut aged just 16 and after being named the SPFA Young Player of the Year in 1979, Stewart once again courted interest.

It took a record fee for a teenage footballer to convince the Tangerines to cash in on their star asset, with a determined John Lyall thrilled to bring Stewart south to the Hammers, having seen his initial bids rejected. Stewart's debut for the Irons was an early birthday present, coming three days before he turned 20. Unfazed, by the end of the season he was celebrating again, the proud owner of an FA Cup winners' medal.

His first goal came early in the 1979/80 campaign. Unsurprisingly, for the man who has scored more penalties than anybody else for the club, it came from the spot, Stewart netting the winner in a 2-1 victory over Burnley. The fact that Stewart took over penalty responsibilities at such a young age and so soon into his Boleyn career spoke volumes and he shouldered it brilliantly.

STEWART

On route to lifting the FA Cup in 1980, two Stewart strikes, including one from the spot, were required to see the team past Orient in the fourth round, but it was his penalty under pressure in the quarter-final that really stood out, stepping up in the dying minutes to cooly blast home the only goal of the game against Aston Villa.

FULL NAME:
Raymond Struan McDonald Stewart

POSITION:
Defender

DATE OF BIRTH:
7 September 1959

PLACE OF BIRTH:
Stanley, Scotland

WEST HAM UNITED DEBUT:
4 September 1979

APPEARANCES:
432

GOALS:
84

West Ham barely had the chance to draw breath during Stewart's second season. He scored penalties in four separate competitions, including in the League Cup Final to force a replay against Liverpool.

The Irons lost the rematch at Villa Park, but continued their march to the Division Two title, Stewart not only contributing with important strikes, but helping stop them at the other end too as part of a frugal defence that only conceded 29 goals all season.

At the end of the domestic season, Stewart received his first full Scottish cap against Wales in the Home Championships. He scored against Northern Ireland four days later and in the same month featured again as Scotland beat England 1-0 at Wembley.

Playing against Stewart that day was Alvin Martin, so often his Hammers partner. The pair had begun 1980/81 under the twin towers in the Charity Shield and Stewart's latest appearance, added to an early appearance for Scotland U15s, took his Wembley total to five.

A strong leader and willing stand-in skipper when required, Stewart's dead-eye penalties continued to win points once back in the top flight. His goal-scoring hit double figures in four different seasons and during December 1982 and January 1983, he netted from twelve yards in four consecutive games. Stewart's final goal for the Hammers came against Norwich City at Carrow Road in December 1988 and again, almost inevitably, it came from the spot. In total, Stewart stepped up 86 times, missing only ten.

STEWART

The following month, he suffered a horrific injury. He did come back to play a part in the closing stages of the 1990/91 Division Two promotion campaign, but returned to Scotland at the end of the season, turning out for St Johnstone and Stirling Albion.

A year and two days after his final league game for the Hammers, 'Tonka' returned to the Boleyn Ground one last time for his testimonial game where Ipswich Town were the visitors.

...forever
blowing bubbles